"Stephen Olford has not only spent his life preaching beautiful expository sermons, he is a peerless teacher of preachers. The Stephen F. Olford Biblical Preaching Library provides substantive examples on how to do it. It will be a great help to many preachers."

Dr. R. Kent Hughes, Senior Pastor
College Church, Wheaton, Illinois

"Stephen Olford is a master expositor and genius at outline clarity. . . . Most preachers can neither walk across the street or travel across the continent to hear him. But they can glean the treasures of his preaching life from The Stephen F. Olford Biblical Preaching Library. I heartily commend this resource."

Dr. Maxie E. Dunham, Senior Pastor
Christ United Methodist Church, Memphis, Tennessee

"Every informed preacher of the Word of God knows of the spiritual power, impeccable scholarship, and practicality of the materials produced by Stephen Olford. Without reservation, I commend The Stephen F. Olford Biblical Preaching Library."

Dr. Adrian Rogers, Senior Pastor
Bellevue Baptist Church, Cordova, Tennessee

Books in the Stephen F. Olford Biblical Preaching Library

Biblical Answers to Personal Problems
Committed to Christ and His Church
Fresh Lessons from Former Leaders
The Pulpit and the Christian Calendar 1
The Pulpit and the Christian Calendar 2
The Pulpit and the Christian Calendar 3
Believing Our Beliefs
Living Words and Loving Deeds

Believing Our Beliefs

*Preaching on the Foundations and
Evidences for New Life*

Stephen F. Olford

BAKER BOOK HOUSE
Grand Rapids, Michigan 49516

Printed in the United States of America

These resources were adapted from material published by the Institute for Biblical Preaching, Box 757800, Memphis, TN 38175-7800.

The New King James Version is used as the basis for Part 1; the King James Version for Part 2. Other versions occasionally used are the Revised Version (RV) and the New English Bible (NEB).

The author is grateful to the many copyright owners for the use of their material.

Contents

Introduction   7

Part 1: Christian Evidence

1. Why I Believe in the Fact of God (Genesis 1:1; John 1:1–4; 1 John 1:1–3)   11
2. Why I Believe in the Son of God (John 1:1–14; Colossians 2:8–12; Hebrews 1:1–2; 1 Timothy 3:16)   20
3. Why I Believe in the Word of God (2 Timothy 3:14–17; 1 Peter 1: 22–25; 2 Peter 1:19–21)   29

Part 2: New Life for You

4. The Seed of the New Life (1 Peter 1:13–2:3)   41
5. The Source of the New Life (John 10:1–11)   49
6. The Start of the New Life (John 3:1–16; 7:50; 19:39)   55
7. The Seal of the New Life (Ephesians 1:3–14; 4:29–32; 5:15–21)   61
8. The Song of the New Life (Psalm 40:1–4)   67

9. The Sense of the New Life (John 10:14–18,
   26–30)   73
10. The Signs of the New Life (1 John 2:29; 3:9; 4:7;
    5:1, 4, 18)   80
11. The Steps of the New Life (Romans 6:1–14)   86
12. The Strength of the New Life (Philippians
    4:1–13)   94
13. The Scope of the New Life (2 Peter 3:1–14)   100

Endnotes   107
For Further Reading   109

Introduction

Believing our beliefs presupposes a threefold basis of faith: belief in the fact of God, belief in the Son of God, and belief in the Word of God. This quintessence of truth is the key that opens up the rest of Scripture.

The Bible starts with the *fact* of God—"In the beginning God . . ." (Gen. 1:1)—and so must we. Indeed, the writer to the Hebrews categorically states this: "Without faith it is impossible to please Him, for he who comes to God must believe that He is, and that He is a rewarder of those who diligently seek Him" (Heb. 11:6).

Then we consider the *Son* of God. Only in him is God revealed to men. John affirms that "no one has seen God at any time. The only begotten Son, who is in the bosom of the Father, He has declared Him" (John 1:18). And Jesus declared, "He who has seen Me has seen the Father" (John 14:9).

This brings us to the *Word* of God. The incarnate Word, in the good providence of God, has become the inscribed Word. The high and holy one has chosen to disclose his person and purpose in human language so that through "the holy scriptures [we are made] . . . wise unto salvation through faith . . . in Christ Jesus" (2 Tim. 3:15, KJV).

The second part of this resource book deals with the

subject of *life.* In a sense, this is the message of the Bible—especially the New Testament. Count the number of times the word "life" occurs in the Gospel of John! The evangelist begins with that glorious announcement: "In Him was life, and the life was the light of men" (1:4). Halfway through his twenty-one chapters he quotes one of the greatest statements our Savior ever made: "I have come that [men and women might] . . . have life, and that they [might] . . . have it more abundantly" (10:10). John concludes his account with words that define the stated purpose of the Gospel: "These are written that you may believe that Jesus is the Christ, the Son of God, and that believing you may have life in His name" (20:31). There we have it. Life and life more abundant is our message to sinners and saints alike. For sinners, because they are "dead in trespasses and sins" (Eph. 2:1) and they need life; for saints, because there is no limit to fullness of life in Christ!

The pages that follow are rich with substance and suggestions to share with those who are ready to believe our beliefs and live the new life in Christ.

Stephen F. Olford

Part 1

Christian Evidence

Why I Believe in the Fact of God
Genesis 1:1; John 1:1–4; 1 John 1:1–3

"In the beginning God . . ." (Gen. 1:1).

Introduction

Dr. W. H. Fitchett in his book on *The Beliefs of Unbelief* says that "God cannot be packed into a syllogism, or 'proved' in terms of logic." Then he adds: "But neither can anyone prove, in terms of logic, that the world exists, or that we ourselves exist! The three final postulates of thought are God, the world, and ourselves; and they are all incapable of absolute metaphysical proof. [The man] who limits his belief to that which can be demonstrated, in terms of formal logic, must deny them all; and all, as a matter of fact have been denied."

In the light of such a statement as this, our demand for logical proof that "God . . . is, and that He is a rewarder of those who diligently seek Him" (Heb. 11:6) is absurd. And yet because men are what they are there will always be an insistence for evidence of what the Christian believes. Perhaps this is why Peter charged the scattered and persecuted Hebrew Christians to "sanctify the Lord God in [their] . . . hearts, and always be ready to give a defense to everyone" for the hope that was in them (1 Peter 3:15). Similarly, if we are asked why we believe in the fact of God we must be ready to give an answer also.

There is a threefold reason for belief in the fact of God:

I. The Recognized Arguments of Natural Reasoning

Among the many arguments that could be advanced there are three that are simple and straightforward:

A. The Cosmological Argument

Otherwise known as the deductive argument, it is the argument of cause and effect.

Kosmos, which is the Greek word for "world," denotes order, arrangement, ornament, and adornment. We cannot stand back, then, and observe this order and arrangement without postulating some great initial cause. There must have been a beginning to the phenomena that we see before us, for science teaches us that the present universe has not existed from all eternity. When we turn to the Bible, the explanation is stated quite clearly and categorically. The writer to the Hebrews says: "By faith we understand that the worlds were framed by the word of God, so that the things which are seen were not made of things which are visible" (Heb. 11:3). Here is a statement which suggests that there is nothing haphazard or accidental in the coming into being of the cosmic order.

B. The Teleological Argument

This is Paley's well-known argument from design. Experience has taught us that whatever is composed of parts requires a designer, and who can that designer be but God?

To quote Dr. Fitchett again: "The absolute proof of God's existence is found in the relations in which the mindless elements of the universe are set with each other, producing an order of which they are not only incapable, but unconscious."

No one can study this supernatural design, and the beauty in the universe around us, without thinking of the apostle's words in Romans 1:20: "For since the creation of the world His invisible attributes are clearly seen, being understood by the things that are made, even His eternal power and Godhead." The majesty, power, and divinity of God are stamped on the creation around us in design and beauty.

Beauty in animals and birds in a measure may be explained, but how shall we account for the beauty of inorganic nature—the sky, the sea, and the flaming sunset? Surely, beauty is the very signature of God. No wonder the psalmist exclaims, "The heavens declare the glory of God; and the firmament shows His handiwork" (Ps. 19:1). And Jesus said, "Consider the lilies of the field, how they grow: they neither toil nor spin; and yet I say to you that even Solomon in all his glory was not arrayed like one of these" (Matt. 6:28–29). Indeed, the one who paints the sunset, who suspends the rainbow in the sky, and colors and scents the petals of the rose, is the God of creation.

C. The Anthropological Argument

This is the moral argument which infers the moral nature of God from the moral nature of man. *Anthropos* is the Greek word for man. The question is, Where did our moral nature come from? Surely our possession of it argues for the existence of a moral governor to whom man is responsible. This argument has been universally admitted by people of all lands.

Among the oldest nations known—the Sumerians and the Egyptians—the evidence, such as it is, shows that monotheism was the earliest faith. Indeed, there is proof that even the paleolithic man was a worshiping creature, though there are no means of knowing what he worshiped. He certainly believed in a future life, as shown by the articles interred with the dead.

The Scriptures make it plain that man, wherever he is found, has an inner monitor which compels belief in God apart from reasoning. Paul tells us that "when Gentiles, who do not have the law, by nature do the things contained in the law, these, although not having the law, are a law to themselves, who show the work of the law written in their hearts, their consciences also bearing witness, and between themselves their thoughts accusing or else excusing them" (Rom. 2:14–15). The sense of right and wrong, and moral responsibility, suggest the intuitive recognition of a moral ruler in the universe.

Illustration

All of this calls to mind the question of God's nature. G. S. Studdert-Kennedy, a British World War I chaplain, tells of visiting a captain who was recovering from what had seemed certain death. He said, "Chaplain, tell me what God is like. Whenever I've been transferred from one regiment to another, my first question has always been, 'What's the colonel like?' because I've discovered that conditions in the regiment will be what the colonel makes them. Before the war, when taking a position with a new firm, I'd always ask, 'What's the boss like?' Now I'm told that I'll recover and live, and I must know what God is like." When we understand the nature of God as being that of complete trustworthiness, all other questions are kept in proper perspective.[1]

II. The Verified Assumptions of Biblical Revelation

The Bible adopts the scientific approach in starting with a hypothesis or assumption. It does not argue for

God, but assumes that God exists, he creates, and he redeems. To believe and act upon these assumptions is to prove that "God . . . is, and that He is a rewarder of those who diligently seek Him" (Heb. 11:6).

A. God Eternally Exists

"In the beginning was the Word, and the Word was with God, and the Word was God. He was in the beginning with God" (John 1:1–2). Here is the clearest statement in the Bible concerning the eternity of God. The phrase, "in the beginning," goes back into the mists and mysteries of an eternity past. If this be assumed and accepted, then God is above and beyond the universe he has created. He has no need of the world, or of us. He is rich in himself. He is fullness of life. All glory, beauty, goodness, and holiness reside in him. He is sufficient unto himself. He is God. It might be asked, "To what end did he create the world?" The answer is, that it might be the theater of his glory; and man, the witness to that glory. (See Rev. 4:11.)

B. God Exclusively Creates

"In the beginning, God created the heavens and the earth" (Gen. 1:1). Dr. D. E. Hart points out that in the first chapter of Genesis the word *bārāʾ*, which means "created," occurs only three times. The first for matter—"In the beginning, God created the heavens and the earth" (Gen. 1:1); the second for animal life—"God created great sea creatures and every living thing that moves" (Gen. 1:21); the third for man—"God created man in His own image" (Gen. 1:27). Man repeats what has already been created by God; only God exclusively creates. John reminds us that "All things were made through Him, and without Him nothing was made that was made" (John 1:3). The universe is not self-produced. Biological analysis has failed to show that a single particle of matter can transmute itself into vitality of movement. To create is a personal act, and the divine order and activity manifested in creation postulates an absolute being as the first cause of all things. The universe reveals a personal God.

C. God Effectively Redeems

"That which was from the beginning, which we have heard, which we have seen with our eyes, which we have looked upon, and our hands have handled, concerning the Word of life—the life was manifested, and we have seen, and bear witness, and declare to you that eternal life which was with the Father and was manifested to us" (1 John 1:1–2). Here we have the revelation, once again, of the preexistent God who manifested himself in history through his incarnation for the redemption of mankind. Although facts can be collated outside of biblical revelation to prove that God visited this earth in human form, yet the purpose and effectiveness of this advent are limited entirely to the revelation given us in the Bible.

So biblical revelation assumes a God who eternally exists, exclusively creates, and effectively redeems. If we start with these hypotheses and build up the related facts of history, we find the picture is complete. The God of biblical revelation is the God of creation and the God of redemption.

Illustration

If we really accept the concept of God as Creator and Redeemer, then we should have no misgivings about allowing him to do with us what pleases him. Some years ago a South American company purchased a printing press from a company based in the States. After the machine reached its destination and had been assembled, workers could not get it to operate properly. Experts tried to remedy the situation, but to no avail. Finally the company wired a message to the manufacturer, asking for a representative of theirs to come to South America and adjust the equipment. Sensing the urgency of the request, the United States firm chose the person who had designed the press. When he arrived, the South American officials were skeptical because he was so young, so they cabled the manufacturer to send a more experienced person. The reply came back, "He made the machine. Let him fix it!"[2]

God made the world and all that is in it. We can do no better than to let him fix it.

III. The Personalized Affirmations of Spiritual Relationship

"Because you are sons, God has sent forth the Spirit of His Son into your hearts, crying out, 'Abba, Father!'" (Gal. 4:6). The most amazing thing about this God in whom we believe is that he has condescended in grace to make it possible for men and women to be related to him by the miracle of the new birth. Sons of Adam's race can be possessors of the divine nature and look up into God's face, saying "Father."

Jesus declared this great fact to one of the leading theologians of his day. The master expressed surprise that Nicodemus was unaware of this fact, since it was implicit and explicit in the Old Testament Scriptures. The Lord said through the prophet Ezekiel: "'I will give you a new heart and put a new spirit within you; I will take the heart of stone out of your flesh and give you a heart of flesh'" (Ezek. 36:26). And Jesus said to Nicodemus: "Do not marvel that I said to you, 'You must be born again'" (John 3:7). This life from above creates a relationship with God which is:

A. Indissoluble

Speaking through his Son, God says concerning his sheep: "I give them eternal life, and they shall never perish; neither shall anyone snatch them out of My hand" (John 10:28). And Paul was persuaded that "neither death nor life, nor angels nor principalities nor powers, nor things present nor things to come, nor height nor depth, nor any other created thing, [can] . . . separate us from the love of God which is in Christ Jesus our Lord" (Rom. 8:38–39).

B. Incomparable

There is no relationship on earth to be compared with the one which exists between God and his people. David said: "When my father and my mother forsake me, then the LORD will take care of me" (Ps. 27:10). And Isaiah asked, "Can a woman forget her nursing child, and not have compassion on the son of her womb? Surely they may forget, yet I will not forget you" (Isa. 49:15). What a comforting thought!

C. Ineffable

So sweet and wonderful is this relationship that Old Testament saints, New Testament Christians, and men and women throughout the ages have shared in the joy of calling God their very own. Listen to the satisfied affirmations that spring from a spiritual relationship with God. Job calls God "my Redeemer" (see Job 19:25), David calls God "my shepherd" (see Ps. 23:1), Solomon calls God "My beloved" (Song of Sol. 2:16), Thomas calls him "My Lord and my God!" (John 20:28), and Paul sums up these expressions of relationship by saying, "My God shall supply all your need" (Phil. 4:19). Such verses as these strengthen our belief in the fact of God.

Illustration

It is one thing to be presented with the facts and quite another to receive them. The story is told of a Burmese prince who had a conversation with a visitor from Europe. The visitor told the prince that in Europe there are rivers that get so hard a person can walk across them in the wintertime. The prince had never seen ice or snow and had never even experienced a cold day. So he could not be persuaded that the visitor was telling the truth. He said, "Though the whole world tell me it is so, I will not believe that a river can get so hard that a person can walk across it." The facts had been presented to him, but he refused to believe.

Conclusion

We have seen that from the recognized arguments of natural reasoning, the verified assumptions of biblical revelation, and the personalized affirmations of spiritual relationship that there is every ground for a personal faith in a personal God. Do you believe in the fact of God?

2

Why I Believe in the Son of God
John 1:1–14; Colossians 2:8–12;
Hebrews 1:1–2; 1 Timothy 3:16

"God was manifested in the flesh" (1 Tim. 3:16).

Introduction

It is believed that the original Christian confession consisted of three words: "Jesus Christ—Lord." We cannot approach the subject of Christianity without believing in the Lord Jesus Christ as the Son of God. His person, claims, and work are central to biblical literature and theology and to all Christian experience. There are three reasons for believing in Christ as the Son of God:

I. His Appearance in History

"God was manifested in the flesh" (1 Tim. 3:16). Professor Carnegie Simpson has said: "If the being of God is beyond your ken, the fact of Christ is not. He is a fact of history, cognizable as any other phenomenon." In other words, Christ has appeared in history, as is evidenced by:

A. Recorded Historical Events

There is secular and scriptural testimony to the fact that Jesus of Nazareth lived over 1900 years ago in the small country of Palestine.

1. THE SECULAR TESTIMONY

Sir J. G. Fraser, who will not be suspected of any bias toward Christianity, once said: "My theory assumes the historical reality of Jesus of Nazareth as the great religious and moral Teacher who founded Christianity and was crucified at Jerusalem, under the governorship of Pontius Pilate. The testimony of the gospels, confirmed by the hostile evidence of Tacitus and younger Pliny, appears amply sufficient to establish these facts to the satisfaction of all unprejudiced inquirers."

2. THE SCRIPTURAL TESTIMONY

There is ample New Testament material to satisfy the keenest of ancient and modern critics, but we shall limit ourselves to two verses from 1 Corinthians, a book which no historical critic can doubt. Here Paul sums up the appearance of Christ in history as follows: "Christ died for our sins according to the Scriptures, . . . He was buried, and He rose again the third day according to the Scriptures" (1 Cor. 15:3–4). In that statement Paul presupposes and includes the birth, life, death, resurrection, and ascension of Jesus Christ.

From the secular and scriptural testimonies, therefore, there is sufficient evidence to lead us to believe in the fact of the incarnation, which is the foundation of Christianity; and the fact of the resurrection, which is the completion of the incarnation and the keystone of the arch of Christianity. Here we have Christ appearing in history as an indisputable fact—one which demands a reasonable belief.

B. Resultant Historical Events

Among them are four:

1. THE CHRISTIAN CHURCH

The church has been here for nearly two millenniums. Its origin can be traced historically to the period when Christ appeared in Palestine.

2. THE CHRISTIAN ORDINANCES

Baptism and the breaking of bread have been observed since the life and death of a man called Jesus of Nazareth.

3. THE CHRISTIAN SUNDAY

This is not the same as the Jewish Sabbath. That was the seventh day of the week. Sunday is the first day of the week and Christians observe that day in honor of our Lord's resurrection.

4. THE CHRISTIAN EASTER

This yearly festival, kept in five continents, can be associated with the same historical time and circumstances: Friday, to commemorate the crucifixion; and Sunday, the resurrection.

Such resultant historical events presuppose and substantiate the appearance of the Lord Jesus Christ in history, and satisfy any honest inquirer who is prepared to believe.

Illustration

Ralph Waldo Emerson has said, "The name of Jesus is not so much written as plowed into the history of the world." And men never tire of reading about him.[1]

II. His Aloneness in History

To quote Professor Simpson again: "Jesus Christ is beyond all reasonable question the greatest Man who ever lived." Instinctively, therefore, we do not class him with others. Jesus is not one of the group of the world's great ones. We can talk about Alexander the Great, Charles the Great, and Napoleon the Great, but Jesus is greater. He is not Jesus the Great, but Jesus the Only! He stands out in his aloneness and uniqueness from other men, yet he was a real man.

Charles Lamb once said: "If Shakespeare were to come into this room we should all rise up to meet him. But if Christ were to come into it, we should all fall down and try to kiss the hem of his garment."

Observe Christ's claim to:

A. Absolute Deity

We cannot read the Gospels without encountering his claim to deity in:

1. THE WORDS HE ACCENTED

Think of three instances in John's Gospel alone concerning the claim he made to objective personal existence prior to the foundation of the world: "Before Abraham was, *I am*" (John 8:58). Then in his great high priestly prayer he said, "Father, glorify Me . . . with the glory which I had with You before the world was" (John 17:5). Since it might be said he could have existed with God before the foundation of the world as a created being, we quote another utterance where he claimed co-equality and co-eternity with the Father—"I and My Father are one" (John 10:30).

2. THE WORKS HE ACCOMPLISHED

Here we are not focusing on the miracles performed in the days of his flesh (similar miracles were done by

Old Testament saints and later by the apostles), but rather on those works of creation, preservation, and redemption. John 1:3 tells us: "All things were made through Him, and without Him nothing was made that was made" (see also Col. 1:16). The eternal Son was the active cause of all creation.

Concerning the work of preservation, we read that, as the Son of God, Jesus Christ was "before all things, and in Him all things consist" (Col. 1:17; see also Heb. 1:3).

As for redemption, this is a work which transcends all others in magnitude and importance, and everywhere in Scripture it is ascribed to Christ (see Heb. 9:11–12).

3. THE WORSHIP HE ACCEPTED

The Lord Jesus, unlike his disciples, always accepted worship, proving that he was on an equality with God (cf. Acts 10:26). When a woman came and worshiped him, saying, "Lord, help me," he did not rebuke her but said, "O woman, great is your faith! Let it be to you as you desire" (Matt. 15:25–28). Thomas, convinced of the identity of the Lord Jesus in that upper room, cried, "My Lord and my God!" (John 20:28). Later, we read that the eleven disciples went away into Galilee, to a mountain where Jesus had appointed them, "and when they saw Him, they worshipped Him" (Matt. 28:16–17). Speaking of his Son, God says, "Let all the angels of God worship Him" (Heb. 1:6). Paul sums up the absolute deity of the Son of God in one of the most profound statements in all the Bible: "In Him dwells all the fullness of the Godhead bodily" (Col. 2:9).

B. Absolute Purity

The greatness of a man is estimated by two things: first, by the purity and dignity of his character; second, by the extent of his influence among mankind. Tried by both these tests, Jesus is supreme among men. He could face friends, foes, and fiends and say, "Which of you convicts Me of sin?" (John 8:46). No wonder a writer of great insight stated that the solitariness and splendor of Christ's character centered in his sinlessness. Paul could say, "He . . . knew no sin" (2 Cor. 5:21). And John could write: "In Him there is no sin" (1 John 3:5). And Peter declared that he "committed no sin" (1 Peter 2:22). Even the infidel Strauss had to confess: "Jesus had a conscience unclouded by the memory of any sin." Such sinlessness was the holiness and goodness of his life which impacted people during his ministry, and does so even to the present day.

Illustration

Socrates taught for 40 years, Plato for 50, Aristotle for 40, and Jesus for only 3. Yet the influence of Christ's three-year ministry infinitely transcends the impact left by the combined 130 years of teaching from these men who were among the greatest philosophers of all antiquity. Jesus painted no pictures; yet, some of the finest paintings of Raphael, Michelangelo, and Leonardo da Vinci received their inspiration from him.

Jesus wrote no poetry; but Dante, Milton, and scores of the world's greatest poets were inspired by him. Jesus composed no music; still Haydn, Handel, Beethoven, Bach, and Mendelssohn reached their highest perfection of melody in the hymns, symphonies, and oratories they composed in his praise. Every sphere of human greatness has been enriched by this humble carpenter of Nazareth.[2]

C. Absolute Sovereignty

The outstanding evidence of his absolute sovereignty was expressed when he said, "I lay down My life that I may take it again. . . . I have power to lay it down, and I have power to take it again" (John 10:17–18). No one before or since Christ has been able to say that. His sovereignty stands alone and unique. In his ability to dismiss his spirit in death and assume his spirit in resurrection is included every other power which the Lord Jesus demonstrated in thought, word, and deed here upon earth.

This unique aloneness of Jesus Christ compels us to choose between the only other two alternatives—both of which are unthinkable. Jesus was either an imposter or he was demented. His sinlessness precludes the idea that he was an imposter, and his amazing influence on subsequent history makes absurd the idea that he was insane. If, therefore, he was neither a fraud nor a lunatic, he must have been what he claimed to be: God incarnate.

Illustration

The story is told of a Frenchman who came to Talleyrand and asked, "Why is it that everybody laughs at my religion?" After explaining his system of religion to Talleyrand, he claimed, "My religion is better than Christianity. What can I do to spread it through the world?" The wiser man replied, "You can live and die serving the people, then on the third day rise from the dead to confirm the hope of humanity, then the people will listen to you." Talleyrand understood that only the Christ can claim sovereignty through the resurrection.

III. His Authority in History

Ever since Christ was in the world men have never been able to rid themselves of the feeling that in him—if in anyone at all—is the quest of faith most likely to find its answer. All who have considered the reality of Jesus Christ have had to admit with Peter, "Lord, to whom shall we go? You have the words of eternal life" (John 6:68). He is irresistibly authoritative in history. As the authoritative Son of God he has:

A. Power to Search Men and Women

"I, the Lord, search the heart, I test the mind, even to give every man according to his ways, and according to the fruit of his doings" (Jer. 17:10). Christ is a fact of conscience. We cannot think of him without being examined ourselves, interrogated authoritatively, reviewed even to our innermost minds, hearts, and wills. We study Aristotle and are intellectually edified; we study Jesus and are in the profoundest way spiritually disturbed. If we search to know him we soon feel his eyes, which are as a flame of fire, piercing us through and through (Rev. 1:14).

B. Power to Save Men and Women

Jesus put forth certain claims which no other man would dare to make. He claimed to have authority to forgive sins. This was made clear on the occasion when he cured the paralytic at Capernaum. His words were: "The Son of Man has power on earth to forgive sins" (Matt. 9:6). No one has turned in genuine repentance to the Son of God for forgiveness and found him to fail. He alone, as the God-man, has the word which is both authoritative and saving. No one who has ever heard that word spoken to their soul can fail to believe in Jesus Christ as the Son of God.

C. Power to Satisfy Men and Women

Nature is benign and beautiful but it gives no answer to your faith. History is but a disappointing and dubious murmur of voices. Look within yourself and you will only find contradiction and confusion. But turn to Jesus Christ and faith always meets its answer. Only Christ can authoritatively say to weary and restless mankind: "Come to Me, all you who labor and are heavy laden, and I will give you rest" (Matt. 11:28).

It was a German author of deep insight who said of Christ that "He knew no more sacred task than to point men and women to His own person." This matchless Savior and Son of God is still doing that today! The hymnist put it perfectly when he said:

Friends all around me are trying to find
What the heart yearns for, by sin undermined;
I have the secret, I know where 'tis found:
Only true pleasures in Jesus abound.
        All that I want is in Jesus;
        He satisfies, joy He supplies;
        Life would be worthless without Him,
        All things in Jesus I find.[3]

Harry Dixon Loes

Conclusion

Criticism may attempt to banish—and the church to bury—his authority, but he always emerges as the authoritative Christ to search, save, and satisfy men and women. That is why countless people believe in Christ as the Son of God; indeed, it is impossible to do otherwise in the light of his appearance in history, his aloneness in history, and his authority in history. In this threefold way Christ appeals to the whole of man's personality. His appearance in history challenges the mind, his aloneness challenges the heart, and his authority challenges the will, and belief is born. Hallelujah, what a Savior!

Why I Believe in the Word of God

2 Timothy 3:14–17; 1 Peter 1:22–25;
2 Peter 1:19–21

"The word of the Lord abideth for ever. And this is the word of good tidings which was preached unto you" (1 Peter 1:25, RV).

Introduction

Someone once said that even though heaven, earth, the visible church, and man himself, crumbled into nonentity, he would, through grace, hold on to the Word of God as the unbreakable link between his soul and God. That man believed the Bible—and so must we, in a day of human speculation and hopeless uncertainty.

Our text teaches that the Bible claims for itself (1) infallibility, for it is "the word of the Lord"; (2) indestructibility, for it "abides for ever"; and (3) indispensability, for it is "the word of good tidings which is preached unto [men]." Let us consider this threefold basis for belief in the Bible:

I. The Infallibility of the Bible

"The word of the Lord . . ." (1 Peter 1:25). By infallibility we are not implying that all the actions recorded in the Bible have divine approval, nor that the words reported have divine authority. In other words, we do not defend Jacob's deception of his father, nor David's sins of immorality and murder. Nor do we mean that the present-day translations and renderings of the original autographs are faultless, for anyone familiar with translations will admit that there have been discrepancies in the medium of expression. At the same time, it is important to note that over 1,150 Old Testament manuscripts exist in the original language that have been examined by Hebrew scholars and proved to be in agreement with each other on all essential points. The number is even higher for New Testament manuscripts.

With that negative backdrop we can positively state that "the word of the Lord"—the Bible—is:

A. God's Infallible Record to Men

"The word of the Lord . . ." (1 Peter 1:25). Note the Bible's claims for itself. It is a record which is:

1. DIVINELY INSPIRED

"All Scripture is given by inspiration of God" (2 Tim. 3:16). Inspiration has been defined as "the supernatural activity of God on the human mind by which the apostles, prophets, and sacred writers were qualified to set forth divine truth without any mixture of error."

The validity of this definition can be illustrated by *the miracle of the Bible's unity.* The Bible was written over a period of 1,500 years by nearly forty authors of different backgrounds. It was penned in three distinct languages—Hebrew, Aramaic, and Greek—in countries far apart; yet the entire book is a harmonious whole. Dr. R. A. Torrey says that "the

Bible is not a superficial unity, but a profound unity." Such unity in diversity can only be accounted for by the fact that the Bible has one author—the Holy Spirit.

Then there is *the miracle of the Bible's accuracy.* Take one instance alone. There are 333 prophecies concerning Christ which have been fulfilled to the letter. By the law of probability, there is only one chance in eighty-three billion that 333 prophecies could be fulfilled in one person. How do we account for the accuracy and dependability of the Old Testament prophecies concerning Christ? The answer is the Holy Spirit (see Acts 1:16).

2. DIVINELY INDITED

"Holy men of God spoke as they were moved by the Holy Spirit" (2 Peter 1:21). Such men were so impelled by the power of the Holy Spirit, above and beyond their times, that they were able to see, hear, and record things quite outside the realm of human imagination. Under such control, fallible men became infallible and faultless in the act of speaking or writing—sometimes even unconsciously, as in the case of Caiaphas when he prophesied of the death of Christ (see John 11:49–52); or Balaam, when he blessed the children of Israel, instead of cursing them (see Num. 23–24).

3. DIVINELY IMPRINTED

"Beginning at Moses and all the Prophets, He expounded to them in all the Scriptures the things concerning Himself" (Luke 24:27). The Bible was not only inspired by God the Father, indited by God the Holy Spirit, but also imprinted by God the Son. He put his stamp of authority not only on the Old Testament Scriptures, but also on the New Testament record that was yet to be written. St. Augustine once said: "Jesus is latent in the Old Testament, and patent in the New." Christ set his imprint on every page (see John 9:39; John 14:26; John 16:13). Therefore, we cannot accept less of that which he inspires, indites, and imprints.

B. God's Infallible Rule for Men

"The word of the Lord . . ." (1:25). Many think the Bible should be an authority on every subject, but this is essentially wrong. The Bible was never intended to teach knowledge which men, by patient labor, may obtain for themselves. For example, the Bible was never intended to be an authority on science. It was Sir Charles Marston who categorically asserted that "there are no contradictions between facts stated in the Scriptures and facts that have been ascertained and brought to light in any department of literary and scientific research." The Bible was never intended to be an authority on philosophy, though this wonderful book contains sound philosophy. Moreover, the Bible was never intended to be an authority on history though no other book gives such an accurate record of human history and the true character of the heart of man. In the last analysis, the Bible was intended to be an infallible record to men and an infallible rule for men in all matters of faith and practice. For this reason, the church has acknowledged the supreme authority of the Bible as God's written Word; as the deposit of the message of salvation; as the "only rule of faith and obedience, teaching what man is to believe concerning God, and what duty God requires of man." Paul sums this up in his great statement in 2 Timothy 3:16–17: "All Scripture is given by inspiration of God, and is profitable for doctrine, for reproof, for correction, for instruction in righteousness, that the man of God may be complete, thoroughly equipped for every good work." In light of this, we may state confidently that the Bible is infallible: it is "the word of the Lord" (1 Peter 1:25).

Illustration

Dr. Robert D. Wilson, former professor of Semitic philology at Princeton Theological Seminary, said, "After . . . years of scholarly research in biblical textual studies and in language study, I have come now to the conviction that no man knows enough to assail the truthfulness of the Old Testament. Where there is sufficient documentary evidence to make an investigation, the statements of the Bible, in the original text, have stood the test."[1]

II. The Indestructibility of the Bible

"The word of the Lord abideth for ever" (1 Peter 1:25 RV). The Bible is indestructible in that it outlives its foes. Jesus said, "Heaven and earth will pass away, but My words will by no means pass away" (Matt. 24:35); and again: "The Scripture cannot be broken" (John 10:35). To believe in the indestructibility of the Bible we need to consider something of the story of:

A. Its Preservation

The Bible contains the oldest books in the world. The first portions were written over 3,000 years ago— nearly a thousand years earlier than any other history we have. Herodotus, one of the oldest historians whose writings are with us today, was contemporary with Ezra and Nehemiah, the last of the historians of the Old Testament. Between these men and Moses there was an interval of nearly a thousand years. Throughout its long history, the Bible has been burned, hidden, criticized, ridiculed, and neglected; yet God has preserved it.

Illustration

Infidels have been at work for centuries firing away at the Bible and making as much impression as you would shooting boiled peas at the Rock of Gibraltar! Voltaire, toward the end of his life, declared that his writings would displace the Bible, and that in 100 years the Word of God would be forgotten. In twenty-five years, the publishing

house which propagated Voltaire's works became the cen-
ter for the Geneva Bible Society, and the ninety beautifully-
bound volumes written against the Bible were sold for pen-
nies apiece. About the same time, one very old copy of an
Old Testament manuscript was sold for thousands of dol-
lars. Truly, "the word of the Lord abideth for ever!"

B. Its Publication

The Bible is never off the printing press. At least one
book of the Bible has been translated into 1,431 languages, the complete Bible into more than 240 languages, and the complete New Testament into more
than 320 languages. For years past, Bibles and New
Testaments have sold at the rate of thirty million copies
a year; that is, fifty every minute. It is by far the world's
best seller. As missionary literature, the Bible has
reached more nations, tribes, and people than any
other book in the world. Missionaries have gone to people with no written language, have caught the significance of words, built an alphabet and grammar, and
put the Bible into that language. This has been done
over 300 times. These statistics are constantly changing
because of the miracle of publication. God has prom-
ised to prosper his Word (see Isa. 55:11).

Illustration

Robert J. Thomas, a Welshman working with the
Scottish Bible Society, yearned to take Bibles to Korea.
His knowledge of the language taught him that Korean is
based on Chinese, and that the educated Koreans could
read it. He boarded an American ship, but a battle broke
out between the ship's officers and the Korean Coast
Guard. The ship was destroyed and all passengers lost.
Before his death, Thomas managed to stagger out of the
water carrying Bibles for Koreans, who clubbed him to
death. Today, Korea has a larger Christian population than
any other Far Eastern country.

III. The Indispensability of the Bible

"This is the word of good tidings which was preached unto you" (1 Peter 1:25, RV). We can do without many books, but we cannot dispense with the Bible. It contains the only word of the gospel for men and women. Within its covers we have an authoritative statement concerning:

A. The Revelation of God

"God, who at various times and in different ways spoke in time past to the fathers by the prophets" (Heb. 1:1). While Christ is the final and authoritative revelation of God, the Bible is the final and authoritative revelation of Christ. John brings these two thoughts together in the 1st and 20th chapters of his gospel. Speaking of Christ as the revelation of God, he says, "No one has seen God at any time. The only begotten Son, who is in the bosom of the Father, He has declared [or expounded] Him" (John 1:18); and again: "These [signs] are written that you may believe that Jesus is the Christ, the Son of God, and that believing you may have life in His name" (John 20:31). Christ is central to the book. Every page of Holy Scripture focuses on him. To encounter Christ is to look into the very face of God, for in the Lord Jesus we have "the brightness of His glory and the express image of His person" (Heb. 1:3). Yes, we can observe the majesty, divinity, and authority of God in creation, but we know nothing of his personal love, mercy, and grace until we meet Jesus Christ.

B. The Redemption of Man

"This is the word of good tidings which was preached unto you" (1 Peter 1:25, RV). Man needs redeeming, but where does one find the plan of redemption? Search the philosophies of men, and the religions of the world, but you search in vain. The Bible says,

"Nor is there salvation in any other, for there is no other name under heaven given among men by which we must be saved" (Acts 4:12).

John Wesley once wrote: "I am a creature of a day, passing through life as an arrow through the air. I am a spirit, coming from God, and returning to God; . . . I want to know one thing—the way to heaven. . . . God Himself has condescended to teach the way. He hath written it down in a book. O give me that book! At any price, give me the book of God!"

In the sweep of redemption, the Bible is indispensable to:

1. Personal Salvation

Writing to young Timothy, Paul reminds him that from childhood he had known the Holy Scriptures. This is the only book able to make a person wise unto salvation through faith in Christ Jesus (see 2 Tim. 3:15). No wonder the Chinese man who had read through the Bible several times admitted, "Whoever made this book made me."

2. Social Integration

Writing to husbands and wives, parents and children, masters and servants, Paul says: "Let the word of Christ dwell in you richly in all wisdom" (Col. 3:16). Only then would husbands love their wives, wives submit to their husbands, children obey their parents, parents provoke not their children to wrath, servants obey their masters and do all things heartily as to the Lord. The sanctity of married life, the security of family life, and the stability of social life are linked to the moral and ethical codes taught in Old and New Testaments.

3. National Reformation

"Righteousness exalts a nation, but sin is a reproach to any people" (Prov. 14:34). The Bible is the only authority on the kind of righteousness that exalts a nation. No other book has to its credit such a record of lives redeemed, moral outcasts regenerated, distressed and anxious souls cheered, and individuals and nations remade. Never has the world known a higher code of ethics. Nor has any other book ever so influenced for good literature, language, art, music, and education. Personal, social, and national prosperity can only come through the preaching of the Word of God.

Illustration

Bruce Buursma, religion editor of the *Chicago Tribune* Press Service, did a write-up entitled "Bible Cure for U.S.: Meese" which appeared in the March 4, 1982 issue of the paper. In it he said: "Presidential Counselor Edwin Meese, a layman in the Lutheran Church-Missouri Synod, told a gathering of conservative Christians here [San Diego] . . . that the Bible holds the answers to the nation's problems. Speaking at the start of a four-day Congress on the Bible, Meese said: 'Nothing is more important in this nation today than this conference on the Bible—not unemployment, not rebuilding our defense capabilities. What is important is rebuilding our relationship to God and a right view of the Bible.' He said: 'There is in our nation a general poverty of the soul. Too many of our people have taken too many wrong roads. We need a reliable road map, and that road map is the Bible.' Meese said President Reagan applauds the involvement of 'Bible-believing Christians' in public policy debates."[2]

Conclusion

If we accept our text then we must believe the Bible is infallible and *learn* it; we must believe the Bible is indestructible and *love* it; we must believe the Bible is indispensable and *live* it.

Part 2

New Life for You

4

The Seed of the New Life
1 Peter 1:13–2:3

"Being born again, not of corruptible seed, but of incorruptible, by the word of God, which liveth and abideth for ever" (1:23, KJV).

Introduction

Our theme for this series of studies is *New Life for You.* There is no more exciting truth in all the range of biblical revelation than that of new life in Christ. It is the essence of the gospel. This is why Christ identified himself with life when he said, "I am . . . the life" (John 14:6). The purpose for which he came into the world was to bring life to those "who were dead in trespasses and sins" (Eph. 2:1). Just as *human* life starts with the seed necessary for physical birth and growth, so *divine* life starts with the seed which brings about spiritual birth and growth. So Peter speaks of "being born again, not of corruptible seed, but of incorruptible, by the word of God, which liveth and abideth for ever" (1:23).

This seed is described as the living and abiding Word of God. Let us examine this a little more closely:

I. The Seed of the New Life Is the Distinctive Word of God

"The word of God, which liveth and abideth for ever . . ." (1:23). The message of new life is not the subject of human speculation, but the substance of divine revelation; it is the Word of God. When we think of the new life we are confronted with four aspects of the Word of God:

A. It Is the Word of Inerrancy

"The word of God, which liveth and abideth for ever . . ." (1:23). Since the Bible reflects the nature and character of an infallible God, we must accept the fact that this Book is divine truth without any admixture of error. Its unity, prophecy, and history prove its inerrancy.

Illustration

In his booklet *Does Inerrancy Matter?*, Dr. James Montgomery Boice tells of two members of the International Council on Biblical Inerrancy who were speaking on a seminary campus at the invitation of the conservative student group. They presented the case for inerrancy as a necessary element for this authority of Scripture, but many of the students objected by denying the need for authority in general. Later, a student wrote to one of the participants in the following manner:

> I have never held to the doctrine of inerrancy, and yet I found myself siding with you as today's discussion proceeded. Is it not true that behind most of the questions you received was a crypto-cultural Christianity; that is, a secret capitulation to the "try it, you'll like it" mentality of our civilization? That is how it seemed to me. Most questioners did not seem to be engaged in a point-for-point argument of any substantial theological

issue. Rather, most seemed to think that to preach the gospel in this day and age one does not need a place to stand. All that one has to do is stand in the pulpit and say, not "Thus saith the Lord," but "Try it, you'll like it."

I am surprised that I found myself feeling that you two were right and all of us were wrong, at least insofar as this very basic point [is concerned]—why we stand where we stand makes all the difference in the world![1]

That quote is extremely revealing and will help you to make your point on inerrancy.

B. It Is the Word of Authority

"The word of God, which liveth and abideth for ever . . ." (1:23). St. Augustine says, "When the Scriptures speak, God speaks," and this is the only way in which we can view the Bible. So as we listen to Scripture we must remember that we are listening to God. We have no right to debate or question what he says. The Bible is the word of authority.

Amplification

Show that in a day of relativism and compromise there is only one way in which we can be sure of what is right and wrong, and that is by listening to the only voice of divine authority, the Word of God.

C. It Is the Word of Eternity

"The word of God, which liveth and abideth for ever . . ." (1:23). Peter reminds us of the words of Isaiah where he says, "All flesh is as grass. . . . The grass withereth, and the flower thereof falleth away: but the word of the Lord endureth for ever" (1:24, 25). Jesus declared, "Heaven and earth shall pass away: but my words shall not pass away" (Mark 13:31). The words of men may fail, but the word of God stands firm for ever. We can depend on what God says. This is why Paul insists that, faced with a choice between man's word versus God's Word, our position must always be: "Let God be true, but every man a liar" (Rom. 3:4).

D. It Is the Word of Vitality

"The word of God, which liveth and abideth for ever
. . ." (1:23). As we shall see, it is the instrument which
the Holy Spirit uses to bring about the miracle of new
life in Christ. We can read the words of man and be
interested and informed, but something supernatural
happens to us when we hear the Word of God. Jesus
said, "The words that I speak unto you, they are spirit,
and they are life" (John 6:63).

The seed of the new life is the distinctive Word of
God. There is something unique and supernatural
about this Book we call the Holy Bible.

II. The Seed of the New Life
Is the Dynamic Word of God

"Being born again, not of corruptible seed, but of incorruptible, by the word of God" (1:23). Inherent in the Word
of God is a dynamic power, and from this passage we find
that:

A. The Word of God Has a Revealing Power
in Jesus Christ

Peter states, "This is the word which by the gospel is
preached unto you" (1:25). Outside of the Bible we
have no gospel, no message for a sin-sick world; but as
we read Holy Scripture we see revealed the only hope
of mankind in Jesus Christ. No other book in all the
world contains the gospel of Jesus Christ. This is why
the Bible is indispensable.

Illustration

Stephen Olford recounts: I will never forget watching the
face of a blind, paramount chief in Angola, Africa as my
missionary father read to him some verses from John's
prologue. Father had just completed the translation of this
portion of Scripture into the A-Chokwe dialect and was try-

ing it out on a man who was totally ignorant of the gospel. As he came to those words, "In him [the Lord Jesus] was life; and the life was the *light of men*" (John 1:4), the chief interjected with a plea—"Say that again, say that again. I am in darkness and I need a light." His face was aglow and his sightless eyes were filled with tears as the simple message of life and light in Christ penetrated his darkness, through the illuminating power of the Holy Spirit. This is what Peter means when he says, "This is the word which by the gospel is preached unto you" (1 Peter 1:25).

B. The Word of God Has a Redeeming Power in Jesus Christ

"Forasmuch as ye know that ye were not redeemed with corruptible things, as silver and gold, from your vain conversation received by tradition from your fathers; but with the precious blood of Christ, as of a lamb without blemish and without spot" (1:18–19).

As we read the Word of God we discover that men and women are slaves to sin. You and I know that this is true; and the central fact of the gospel is that the Lord Jesus came to redeem us at the cost of his own blood by paying the price on Calvary's cross. He made possible our salvation from sin, self, and Satan, as recorded in the Scriptures. So there is a redeeming power in this seed of the Word.

Illustration

Illustrate the redeeming power of the gospel in your own life, or in some other conversion story.

C. The Word of God Has a Renewing Power in Jesus Christ

"Being born again, not of corruptible seed, but of incorruptible, by the word of God, which liveth and abideth for ever" (1:23). As the gospel is read or preached, the spirit of God uses the truth to bring about the miracle known as the new birth. As natural seed falls into the ground, germinates and brings forth life, so the seed of the Word falls into the human heart and spiritual life begins.

Nourished by this same Word, new life grows and matures. Peter puts it simply and clearly when he writes: "As newborn babes, desire the sincere milk of the word, that ye may grow thereby" (2:2).

Amplification

Amplify this by applying the thrust of this truth. Ask your congregation such questions as: Have you been born again? Do you know this new life in Christ? Point out that this miracle can take place even as they listen to the message.

III. The Seed of the New Life Is the Directive Word of God

"Seeing ye have purified your souls in obeying the truth . . . love one another with a pure heart fervently" (1:22). No one can listen to the Word of God and stay neutral. The Bible demands obedience. Failure to obey is disobedience, and disobedience is sin (1 Sam. 15:22–23) judged by God with eternal punishment (2 Thess. 1:8–10). So we must be quick to obey what the Bible teaches. The Bible directs us into three areas of obedience:

A. The Word of God Demands the Obedience of Faith

Peter writes here of "faith . . . in God" (1:21). The Bible never directs us to place our faith in men, in works, or institutions, but rather in God. This calls for repentance, or a change of mind. The reason for this is that our natural tendency is to depend on ourselves or on human resources—and God calls this sin. Repentance is a change of mind which leads to a change of direction and destiny. Faith in God means commitment or surrender to Jesus Christ, because no man can come to God except through Jesus Christ. So we read that "faith cometh by hearing, and hearing by the word of God" (Rom. 10:17).

B. The Word of God Demands the Obedience of Hope

Peter also speaks of "hope . . . in God" (1:21). Outside of the Christian gospel man is utterly hopeless. This is becoming more and more apparent to thoughtful people in the secularized world in which we live. There is no hope in human inventions and institutions. All around us are failure and frustration. We understand why the existentialist describes life as "a long, dark tunnel without an end." Life, he tells us, is an absurdity, a meaningless nightmare. This is the doctrine of despair.

What a relief, therefore, to turn to the gospel of our Lord Jesus Christ and find hope! The Son of God died and rose again to give us hope, and because he lives we can know this living hope in a personal, powerful way.

Amplification

Extend this thought of hope beyond this life to the eschatological outlook for the true believer.

C. The Word of God Demands the Obedience of Love

In "obeying the truth" we are told to "love one another with a pure heart fervently" (1:22). The world knows little about true love. This is why there is so much failure in human relationships in the home, in business, and in society. But the Bible gives us the secret of true love. What we can't do the Holy Spirit can perform in our hearts through this new life in Christ, creating in us active, fervent love to both God and man. The human heart was made for love and will never be satisfied without it. This is why life is meaningless until we come to know new life in Christ.

Illustration

Show how *agape* love transforms human relationships.

Conclusion

We have seen that this new life in Christ starts with a
seed—the Word of God. It is a distinctive Word, trust-
worthy and authoritative. It is a dynamic Word which has
power to reveal, redeem, and renew. It is a directive Word
which demands obedience. To listen to this Word calls for
a verdict. To accept its message is to come into blessing;
to reject its message is to remain in bondage. In the final
analysis, when we refer to the Word we speak not only of
the written Word but also the Living Word, our Lord Jesus
Christ. He is God's seed who longs to be planted and
nourished in our hearts. Are we prepared to accept or
reject him? This is the crucial issue.

5

The Source of the New Life
John 10:1–11

"The thief cometh not, but for to steal, and to kill, and to destroy: I am come that they might have life, and that they might have it more abundantly" (10:10).

Introduction

Thirty-four times or more the word "life" occurs in the Gospel of John. In fact, it is the key word of this book, and we cannot read through its pages without seeing quite clearly that the purpose for which Christ came into this world was to bring life, and life more abundant.

More abundant than what? we ask. Before we go any further, we must define what we mean by this new life in Christ. If we were to walk through a forest and pick a flower we would be touching *vegetable life.* As we proceeded on our walk, our attention might be attracted by a beautiful dog and we would be looking at *animal life.* Later on, we might meet a hunter, coming our way with a gun over his shoulder, and as we greeted him we would

encounter *human life.* Then as we continued we might be
fortunate enough to see a young woman relaxing under a
shady tree, reading her Bible, and after questioning her
we would discover that she possessed *spiritual life,* a life
qualitatively different than vegetable, animal, or human
life. This is what Jesus was talking about when he said, "I
am come that they might have life, and that they might
have it more abundantly." When he gave expression to
this tremendous statement he was declaring himself to be
the source of a new *kind* of life. In him, and in him alone,
can we know this abundant life. In presenting this poten-
tial of life to men and women, Jesus spoke of three important matters that demand our close attention:

I. The Enemies of This New Life in Christ

"The thief cometh not, but for to steal, and to kill, and
to destroy: I am come that they might have life, and that
they might have it more abundantly" (10:10). The enemies, of course, refer to the thieves, robbers, strangers,
and hirelings mentioned in this opening paragraph.
Unfortunately, in many of our churches and pulpits today
are men who are nothing more than thieves and robbers,
holding back that "more abundant" life from hungry and
thirsty people. Satan is out to rob the church of this gift
of abundant life. If he cannot deprive us of the gift of life,
he proceeds to deceive us about the glory of that life. And
so the Master warned us against the enemies of this new
life. He pointed out that

A. The Enemies Are Deceptive in Their Methods

"Verily, verily, I say unto you, He that entereth not
by the door into the sheepfold, but climbeth up some
other way, the same is a thief and a robber" (10:1). Not
only in Christ's day, but in our time there are enemies
of the gospel who insist that there is more than one
door into the sheepfold of God's salvation. But this is a

lie, and we must not be deceived. Jesus said, "I am the door: by me if any man enter in, he shall be saved" (10:9). He also declared, "I am the way . . . no man cometh unto the Father, but by me" (John 14:6).

Illustration

Tell the story of Simon the sorcerer (Acts 8:5–25).

B. The Enemies Are Defective in Their Message

"A stranger will they not follow, but will flee from him; for they know not the voice of strangers" (10:5). The voice verbalizes and articulates the identity, reality, and authority of the message that is preached.

Illustration

Explain how the modern voices of liberalism, humanism, communism, etc. fail in their message to redeem man from sin.

C. The Enemies Are Destructive in Their Motives

"The thief cometh not, but for to steal, and to kill, and to destroy" (10:10). Enemies of the gospel don't give; they take. They don't quicken; they deaden. They don't bless; they damn. In other words, they kill, they steal, and they destroy. That last word is strong in the original Greek. It means "to utterly destroy."

Illustration

Explain the various methods that the enemies of the cross use for "climbing up some other way." A good biblical example is the story of Balak (meaning "devastator"). Balak was king of Moab when Israel emerged from the wilderness to enter Canaan. Having seen what the Hebrews had done to the Amorites, he attempted to prevent Israel's advance by hiring Balaam to curse them (see Num. 22:1–6). He built altars at three different sites for the purpose, but each attempt failed. He is remembered throughout biblical history as an example of the folly of attempting to thwart Jehovah's will (see Josh. 24:9; Judg. 11:25).

II. The Certainties of This New Life in Christ

Jesus said, "I am come that they might have life, and that they might have it more abundantly" (10:10). This victorious and continuous life in Christ is not just a philosophy or a theology, it is a person, the Lord Jesus Christ, concerning whom there are certainties that we cannot ignore or escape.

A. This New Life in Christ Is Historically Observable

Jesus said, "I am come that they might have life" (10:10).

Amplification

Show how this life in Christ was manifested by his incarnation, demonstrated by his crucifixion, and vindicated by his resurrection.

B. This New Life in Christ Is Dynamically Obtainable

"I am come that they might have life, and that they might have it more abundantly" (10:10). He also declared: "I give unto them eternal life; and they shall never perish" (10:28). John picks up this great theme in his epistle and says: "And this is the record, that God hath given to us eternal life, and this life is in his Son. He that hath the Son hath life; and he that hath not the Son of God hath not life" (1 John 5:11–12).

Illustration

Illustrate by using three envelopes of different sizes. Label the smallest size *life,* the next size *Christ,* and the largest size *me* or *you.* Put the *life* envelope into the *Christ* envelope, and then insert the *Christ* envelope into the *me/you* envelope. As you do this, quote slowly and emphatically, "And this life is in his Son. He that hath the Son hath life."

III. The Qualities of This New Life in Christ

"I am come that they might have life, and that they might have it more abundantly" (10:10). And again: "The good shepherd giveth his life for the sheep" (10:11). As we examine these tremendous words, notice three things about this new life in Christ; and as we consider each one, challenge your own heart as to whether or not you have personally experienced this quality of life.

A. It Is a New Life Which Is Appealing

"I am come that they might have life" (10:10).

EXEGESIS

Explain the meaning of "the good shepherd" and use Galatians 5:22–23, and other Scriptures, to describe our Lord's beauty and glory.

B. It Is a New Life Which Is Abounding

"I am come that they might have life, and that they might have it more abundantly" (10:10); or, as the New English Bible has it, "I have come that men might have life, and may have it in all its fullness." This is a wonderful thing about the new life in Christ. As the Word of God deepens our capacity, so the Son of God fills that capacity with all his fullness. In him is all the fullness of the Godhead bodily, and we are complete in him (Col. 2:9).

Illustration

The story is told of A. B. Simpson who heard of D. L. Moody's encounter with the Holy Spirit, when, in a moment of time, he seemed to be filled with the very glory of heaven. So he traveled to Chicago to hear the great evangelist preach. Sitting at the back of the auditorium he waited for Moody to come on to the platform. In the meantime, the songleader introduced a hymn with the words, "Isn't it wonderful to know that 'everything is in Jesus, and

Jesus is everything'?" For A. B. Simpson, that was all he
needed to hear. Picking up his briefcase, he left the taber-
nacle and never heard Moody preach on that occasion.
Later he made those words the motto of his ministry:
"Everything is in Jesus, and Jesus is everything; tell the
world as fast as you can!"

C. It Is a New Life Which Is Abiding

"I am come that they might have life, and that they
might have it more abundantly" (10:10). And if we ask
the question, "What kind of life?" the answer is clear
and conclusive: it is eternal life. Jesus said, "This is life
eternal, that they might know thee the only true God,
and Jesus Christ, whom thou hast sent" (John 17:3).
This abiding life does not die when we die physically.
Indeed, physical death is only an open door into a fuller
life in Jesus Christ. This abiding life is eternal because
it begins on earth and continues in heaven. What a glorious gift for those who are prepared to receive it! And
we have learned that the source of this life is Christ
himself, who said: "I am come that they might have life,
and that they might have it more abundantly" (10:10).

Illustration

Illustrate the endlessness or permanence of this life in
Christ, both personally and eschatologically.

Conclusion

Remember the enemies of this new life, the certainties
of this new life, and the qualities of this new life. With
these truths in mind I invite you to receive this new life
in Christ. He is God's "unspeakable gift." To reject him is
to reject life, and to reject life is to perish eternally. Won't
you say, "Thanks be unto God for his unspeakable gift,"
then open the hand and heart of your faith and say "thank
you"?

6

The Start of the New Life
John 3:1–16; 7:50; 19:39

"Except a man be born again, he cannot see the kingdom of God. . . . Except a man be born of water and of the Spirit, he cannot enter into the kingdom of God" (3:3, 5).

Introduction

The greatest message on new life ever delivered by the Lord Jesus Christ was addressed to a deeply religious man named Nicodemus. What is so significant is that this ruler of the Jews, with all his religion, was a very dissatisfied man. Something vital was missing in his life. So we find him coming to one in whom he had recognized a quality of life which transcended the religious formalism of his day. It is evident that Nicodemus longed for this new life in Christ, for he came to find out how he might possess it. In the dialogue which followed, Jesus indicated three conditions for the start of this new life:

I. There Must Be the Sense of Need

Nicodemus said, "Rabbi, we know that thou art a teacher come from God: for no man can do these miracles [these signs of new life] that thou doest, except God be with him" (3:2). In these words Nicodemus was admitting a threefold, basic need that could only be met in Jesus Christ:

A. Man Is Blind in Sin and Therefore Needs New Life

"Except a man be born again, he cannot see the kingdom of God" (3:3). This means that without divine life no one can see or understand the things that pertain to the spiritual realm.

Illustration

Illustrate the solemn truth of 1 Corinthians 2:14 and 2 Corinthians 4:4. Until the eyes of the heart are open, by the revealing power of the Holy Spirit, the natural man can only say, "I don't believe it," or, "I cannot see it," or "It is utter nonsense."

B. Man Is Bound in Sin and Therefore Needs New Life

"Except a man be born again of water and of the Spirit, he cannot enter into the kingdom of God" (3:5). In other words, sin has so bound man in mind, heart, and will to his good works, self-righteousness, religious opinions, and fear of man, that without life from God he cannot break free to enter the kingdom of God.

Illustration

Illustrate how religionism, traditionalism, and even denominationalism can bind men and women in their sin.

C. Man Is Born in Sin and Therefore Needs New Life

"That which is born of the flesh is flesh; and that which is born of the Spirit is spirit" (3:6). And Paul tells us that "flesh and blood cannot inherit the kingdom of God" (1 Cor. 15:50). You see, "that which is begotten carries within it the nature of that which begat it" is an irrevocable law of life.

Illustration

Henry Moorhouse tells of a father and son who were walking down the streets of New York City when they came to a sign which read, "Come inside and see the performing pig." "Oh, Daddy, let's go in," begged the boy. "We haven't time," replied the father—but you can guess who won the argument! When they were seated inside and sufficient people had gathered, the proprietor opened a little door and out came the cleanest looking pig—complete with trousers, waistcoat, and bow tie. When there was silence, the proprietor announced that he was going to ask the pig to form a sentence with some wooden letters on the floor. The pig nosed the letters around until they spelled, "I'm a good pig." By this time the little boy's eyes were like saucers, and looking at the pig, and then at his father, he blurted out, "B-but, it's still a pig, isn't it?" The answer, of course, was "Yes, it's still a pig," with all its cleanness, clothes, and cleverness.

And so Nicodemus, like every son of Adam, was born in sin—in spite of all his education and religious refinements. In consequence, he could not inherit the kingdom of God. Is it any wonder that Jesus exclaimed, "Marvel not that I said unto thee, ye must be born again" (3:7).

II. There Must Be the Step of Faith

Addressing this religious leader, Jesus declared, "God so loved the world, that he gave his only begotten Son, that whosoever believeth in him should not perish, but have everlasting life" (3:16). With those glorious words that contain the core of the gospel, Jesus emphasized that this new life is not merited or inherited by human means: rather, it is the gift of God to be received by faith. For this to happen:

A. The Spirit Must Produce This New Life

"The wind bloweth where it listeth, and thou hearest the sound thereof, but canst not tell whence it cometh, and whither it goeth: so is every one that is born of the Spirit" (3:8). Man can no more control life from above than he can govern the light breezes in the treetops. It is the sovereign power and prerogative of the Holy Spirit alone to produce this new life in those who are sensitive to his prompting. This is why it is so serious to resist him when he strives with us. To refuse his offer may mean the damning of our souls. God warns, "My Spirit shall not always strive with man" (Gen. 6:3).

Amplification

Amplify the seriousness of resisting the Spirit of God (see Acts 7:51)

B. The Savior Must Provide This New Life

"As Moses lifted up the serpent in the wilderness, even so must the Son of man be lifted up: that whosoever believeth in him should not perish, but have eternal life" (3:14–15). By this reference to the Old Testament story, Jesus implies that just as Moses lifted up the serpent in the wilderness to show God's answer of life to the sting of death for the snake-bitten Israelites, so, by the lifting up of the Son of man (on the cross and in resurrection), God declared, once and forever, his answer of life to the sentence of death, which is upon all who have sinned and come short of his glory.

Amplification

Amplify the story of Moses and the brazen serpent in the wilderness (Num. 21).

C. The Sinner Must Possess This New Life

"Whosoever believeth in him should not perish, but have eternal life" (3:15). The one who believes in Christ possesses God's life, for "he that hath the Son hath life" (1 John 5:12). The moment Christ is received by faith, the miracle of the new birth takes place. At once the sinner enjoys a new sight, a new liberty, and a new nature in Christ. This is the result of a step of faith.

Illustration

Illustrate this step of faith by relating a clear-cut story of conversion.

III. There Must Be the Sign of Life

Jesus said, "We speak that we do know, and testify that we have seen" (3:11). Jesus was undoubtedly referring to his disciples who had already received this new life in Christ. But, even more important, he was underscoring the necessity of *expressing* this new life in Christ. It is significant that the next two references to Nicodemus in this Gospel describe his confession of Christ before others. In examining the relevant passages, observe two characteristics of this sign of new life in Christ.

A. The Confession of Christ Must Be Fearless

"Nicodemus saith unto them [the religious leaders], (he that came to Jesus by night, . . .) Doth our law judge any man, before it hear him, and know what he doeth? (7:50–51). The context here reveals that the religious leaders had sent officers to apprehend the Savior, but these soldiers had returned without Jesus, saying, "Never man spake like this man" (7:46). The Pharisees were furious at this reaction and expressed themselves accordingly. But in that atmosphere of hostility Nicodemus challenged the whole Sanhedrin as to the fairness of judging anyone before seeing him and hearing him. Here was a clear-cut example of a fearless stand for Christ.

Illustration

Cite instances of fearless confession that you have witnessed.

B. The Confession of Christ Must Be Faithful

"And there came also Nicodemus, which at the first came to Jesus by night, and brought a mixture of myrrh and aloes, about a hundred pound weight. [And] . . . took . . . the body of Jesus, and wound it in linen clothes with the spices, as the manner of the Jews is to bury" (19:39, 40). After Christ had been crucified, two people were concerned that the body should have an honorable burial. One was Joseph of Arimathea, and the other was Nicodemus. So they asked Pilate for permission to perform the burial rites. It was Nicodemus, however, who brought along a hundred pounds of myrrh and aloes to embalm the body, identifying himself forever with the Christ of the cross. We can never think of Calvary without thinking of Nicodemus. By embalming that precious body, Nicodemus publicly symbolized his identification with the death, burial, and resurrection of the Savior. The apostle Paul later described this identification as being "dead and risen with Christ" (Rom. 6). What a splendid testimony Nicodemus gave to this new life in Christ, and how carefully we should remember this when thinking of the man who came to Jesus by night.

This is God's threefold condition for new life in Christ: there must be the sense of need, the step of faith, and the sign of life in Christ.

Conclusion

Do you want to start a new life in Christ? Then emulate Nicodemus. Come as he did, and you will leave as he did.

7

The Seal of the New Life
Ephesians 1:3–14; 4:29–32; 5:15–21

"In whom ye also trusted, after that ye heard the word of truth, the gospel of your salvation: in whom also after that ye believed, ye were sealed with that holy Spirit of promise" (1:13)

Introduction

We all know that no official document is of any value unless it has been notarized. To be valid it must have the stamp or seal of authority. What is true in the commercial world is equally true in the spiritual realm. To be an authentic Christian, a person must have the seal of the Holy Spirit—and this is what Paul is talking about in the passages before us. He was writing to Christians who were familiar with the use of the seal. Ephesus was a seaport which shipped, among other things, large quantities of lumber. When buyers came to purchase this commodity they stamped each beam with their seal so that it could be claimed without question when it reached its destination. The seal was the symbol of ownership and security.

So, writing to the believers, Paul says, "[You] were sealed with . . . [the] holy Spirit of promise" (1:13), and later on he warns them not to grieve the Spirit of God, "whereby [they were] . . . sealed unto the day of redemption" (4:30). Then he concludes his letter by saying, "Be filled with the Spirit" (5:18). From these statements we learn:

I. The Seal of the New Life Is the Possession of the Holy Spirit in Personal Experience

"In whom ye also trusted, after that ye heard the word of truth, the gospel of your salvation: in whom also, after that ye believed, ye were sealed with that holy Spirit of promise" (1:13). For this miracle to take place in personal experience:

A. A Person Must Hear the Word of the Gospel

"In whom ye also trusted, after that ye heard the word of truth, the gospel of your salvation" (1:13). God has ordained that the gospel message should be preached throughout the world to every creature. This explains why every Christian should be a witness, why evangelistic crusades are held, and why local churches are established. Elsewhere Paul tells us that the gospel is the Good News of God's love to men and women who are dead in trespasses and sins. It is the story of how Christ "died for our sins according to the scriptures; and that he was buried, and that he rose again the third day according to the scriptures" (1 Cor. 15:3–4).

Amplification

Show the need for preaching the gospel in every age to all nations (see Matt. 28; Rom. 10:13–14).

B. A Person Must Heed the Lord of the Gospel

"In whom . . . after that ye believed, ye were sealed with that holy Spirit of promise" (1:13). The implication here is quite clear. It is not sufficient to hear the word of the gospel, we must heed, or obey, the Lord of the gospel. Jesus waits to enter our lives, by the power and presence of the Holy Spirit, but we must first obey him in repentance and faith. This means confessing and forsaking our sins, and then placing our trust in the Lord Jesus who died to put away our sins, and rose again to make us right with God. The Bible teaches that when we truly hear the word of the gospel and then heed the Lord of the gospel, a miracle takes place. The Holy Spirit of promise enters our lives and we are sealed forever. God puts his stamp of ownership and security upon us, and no angel in heaven, no man on earth, no demon in hell, can ever break that seal.

Exegesis

Exegete the word "seal" in this context and elsewhere, for example, Matthew 27:66; John 3:33; Romans 15:28, 2 Corinthians 1:22; Revelation 7:3–5; 10:4; 20:3. (William Barclay has some helpful comments in his *Letters to the Ephesians* rev. ed. [Westminster Press, 1975].)

II. The Seal of the New Life Is the Position of the Holy Spirit in Personal Experience

"Grieve not the holy Spirit of God, whereby ye are sealed unto the day of redemption" (4:30). It is quite obvious from this verse that the Holy Spirit is a person who can be grieved and hurt. This happens when we fail to give him his rightful place in our lives as the *Holy* Spirit who has sealed us unto the day of redemption. The purpose of God, through the ministry of the Holy Spirit, is to purify our lives until we become more and more like our

Lord Jesus. This progressive work of the Holy Spirit will not be completed until the day of redemption. In the meantime, however, we must avoid grieving him. In the context of this passage, the apostle shows:

A. What It Means to Give Place to the Devil

"Neither give place to the devil" (4:27). We give place to the devil when we tell untruths (4:25), when we lose our tempers (4:26), when we rob our neighbors (4:28), when we use bad language (4:29), and when we show bitterness of spirit (4:31). In simple terms, we give place to (or accommodate) the devil when we grieve the Holy Spirit by unholy thoughts, words, and deeds. God has called us to holy living, and that is why he has given us the Holy Spirit. Therefore, anything contrary to the nature of a holy God grieves the Spirit.

Illustration

Illustrate with stories of living situations where the devil has had his way in a believer's life.

B. What It Means to Give Place to the Spirit

"Speak every man truth with his neighbour: for we are members one of another" (4:25). We are to be honest with our neighbors (4:25), we are to work hard in our jobs (4:28), we are to show grace in our speech (4:29), and we are to be kind and forgiving to all (4:32). Once again, this simply means accommodating the Holy Spirit, giving him his rightful position in every department of our lives. This is the seal of the new life in Christ—not only in the possession of the Holy Spirit, but the position of the Holy Spirit. It should be evident to all that our lives are controlled by the Spirit of God.

Amplification

Explain what it means to be filled with the Spirit (Eph. 5:18).

III. The Seal of the New Life Is the Provision of the Holy Spirit in Personal Experience

"Be not drunk with wine, wherein is excess; but be filled with the Spirit" (5:18). If God's Spirit is both acknowledged and obeyed in our lives, certain things follow which are described to us in this wonderful passage.

A. A New Melody Comes into Our Lives

"Singing and making melody in your hearts to the Lord" (5:19). Instead of singing the songs of drunkenness and sordidness we are caught up in the psalms, hymns, and spiritual songs of the church, giving thanks to God for all things (5:19–20).

Illustration

Illustrate from stories of revival, how spirit-filled men and women become a singing community.

B. A New Harmony Comes into Our Lives

"Submitting yourselves one to another in the fear of God" (5:21). There will be a harmony in the church between pastor and people, and the whole congregation will love and be loved among its members. There will be a harmony in the home between husbands and wives, parents and children, and the whole family will love and be loved among its members. There will be a harmony in the business between employer and employee because each will love the other. This does not mean that everything will be perfect this side of heaven, but there is no question that relationships grow sweeter and stronger when the Holy Spirit is in control.

Amplification

Amplify the meaning of reciprocal love in the relationships of life.

C. A New Victory Comes into Our Lives

"Be strong in the Lord, and in the power of his might" (6:10). We discover that in spite of the principalities, powers, and rulers of the darkness of this world, in spite of spiritual wickedness in high places arrayed against us, we have an offensive and defensive armor in Jesus Christ that guarantees victory every day of our lives.

Amplification

Amplify by detailing the pieces of armor, both for defensive and offensive spiritual warfare.

D. A New Liberty Comes into Our Lives

"That . . . I may speak boldly, as I ought to speak" (6:20). With Paul the apostle we can testify that through the prayers of God's people and the power of the Holy Spirit we can open our mouths anywhere, at any time, to share the message of the gospel.

Illustration

Show from the Book of the Acts what it means to be bold in Christian witness.

Conclusion

Remember that the seal is a person, the Holy Spirit. We must therefore know by experience his possession, his position, and his provision in our lives. Only then can we call ourselves true Christians. Have you received the Holy Spirit? If not, will you repent right now, believe in the Lord Jesus Christ as your Savior, and then, as an act of faith, ask the person of the Holy Spirit into your life right now?

8

The Song of the New Life
Psalm 40:1–4

"He hath put a new song in my mouth, even praise unto our God" (40:3).

Introduction

We have been created to sing. This explains why a nation has its national anthem, why the armed forces march to the strains of martial music, why a college has its alma mater, and why each of us has a favorite song.

When we come to the Bible, we find that the God of creation and redemption is the God of song. When the universe was brought into existence "the morning stars sang together, and all the sons of God shouted for joy" (Job 38:7). And when God brought his people out of the bondage of Egypt the children of Israel sang the song of Moses (Exod. 15). One day, when God's purposes of redemption are consummated, we are all going to sing the song of the Lamb.

So we see that our singing is an evidence of our life. And no one helps us to understand this better than the psalmist David. He could testify: "He hath put a new song in my mouth, even praise unto our God."

I. This New Song Speaks of a Life of Deliverance

"He brought me up also out of a horrible pit, out of the miry clay" (40:2). Here David is describing in graphic terms what it means to be delivered from the guilt and grip of sin. Whatever historical events occasioned the writing of this psalm is incidental to the basic principle that he is enunciating. This shepherd-king could sing because he knew a twofold deliverance:

A. Deliverance from the Guilt of Sin

"He brought me up also out of a horrible pit" (40:2). The Hebrew reads: "He brought me up out of a pit of noise"—and this is most suggestive. David has in mind the pits that were often dug to capture wolves, bears, or lions, but occasionally thieves and robbers were also trapped this way. The pit was so shaped that every cry for help would echo and reverberate. A trap of this kind was truly a "pit of noise."

How graphically this illustrates the guilt of sin. Until we know the deliverance of God, we are forever haunted by the accusations of the devil, as well as the voice of our self-condemnation.

Illustration
Illustrate in terms of your personal experience.

B. Deliverance from the Grip of Sin

"He brought me up . . . out of the miry clay" (40:2). We are told that the bottom of these pits was often covered with a miry clay, or sticky sediment, which impeded attempts to escape. Indeed, the more the victim struggled to get free, the deeper he sank into the miry clay.

Illustration

Stephen Olford recounts: "I can never think of this psalm without recalling an experience I once had in Angola, West Africa. I arose one morning to hunt a wild goose for our Christmas dinner. As I waited at the rice fields a flock of these birds flew in and I took aim and fired, killing one and wounding another. But as I chased the wounded bird I found myself caught in a bog; the more I fought to free myself, the deeper I sank, and the horror of a ghastly death overwhelmed me. At this point there was nothing I could do but cry for help—and to my utter relief I saw emerging, from the bushes, one of the faithful men who served on our mission compound. Although he was wearing a beautiful native print cloth, he stripped it from his body and threw one end to me. I grasped it with the strength of desperation, and little by little my deliverer drew me safely out of the bog. My struggle was over. A saving hand had been stretched out at the sacrifice of something that was very valuable to my African friend. I could sing a new song. I was alive!"

This is the gospel in a nutshell. Our Lord and Savior Jesus Christ laid aside the glory of heaven in order to save us not only from the guilt of sin, but from the grip of sin. By his death we were reconciled to God, but by his life we are constantly being delivered from the power of the indwelling sin nature. To struggle in our own strength is to sink deeper and deeper into trouble, but to trust the saving life of Christ is to know deliverance day by day.

II. This New Song Speaks of a Life of Direction

"He brought me up also out of a horrible pit, out of the miry clay, and set my feet upon a rock, and established my goings" (40:2). The godless are always described in Scripture as lost. They don't know where they have come

from, where they are, where they are going; but it is quite
different for the Christian. He knows where he stands,
and he also knows where he is going. Direction implies:

A. The Christian's Position in Christ

"He [hath] . . . set my feet upon a rock" (40:2). In this
particular context we are told the Christian is standing
securely on the rock.

Amplification

Amplify the thought of being on the rock as the place of
security (Exod. 33:22), the place of sufficiency (Isa. 32:3;
1 Cor. 10:4), and the place of serenity (Isa. 26:3–4,
marginal rendering).

B. The Christian's Progression in Christ

"He . . . established my goings" (40:2). Long before
the foundations of the world were laid, the God of
foreknowledge planned our lives. One of the most exciting things about the Christian experience is to find,
follow, and finish that plan as we walk the pathway of
obedience.

Amplification

Expound the meaning of Ephesians 2:10.

III. This New Song Speaks of a Life of Devotion

"He hath put a new song in my mouth, even praise
unto our God: many shall see it, and fear, and shall trust
in the LORD" (40:3). This is the climactic thought in the
whole progression of ideas which David shares with us.
Deliverance leads to direction, but direction to devotion.
When we know our salvation in Christ, as well as our
standing in Christ, then and only then can we fully
express our song in Christ. God made us to love him, and
this response finds expression in:

A. *The Devotion of Worship*

"He hath put a new song in my mouth, even praise unto our God" (40:3). "Man's chief end is to glorify God, and to enjoy him forever" states the Westminster Shorter Catechism; therefore, his greatest activity is that of worship. More is said in the Bible about worship than about service.

Illustration

Show from example of Scripture that God desires our worship before he desires our service.

B. *The Devotion of Witness*

"Many shall see it, and fear, and shall trust in the Lord" (40:3). Where there is worship there is also witness. No one can live in the presence of God without reflecting the glory of God. This is what made the early apostles so distinctive and effective in that first-century church.

Illustration

Illustrate from the life and witness of the early apostles, for example, Acts 4:13.

Conclusion

The question arises how this song can begin. David gives the answer. He said: "I waited patiently for the Lord; and he inclined unto me, and heard my cry" (40:1). Literally, the Hebrew idiom is "Waiting I waited for the Lord; and he inclined unto me, and heard my cry." First, there must be *submission*—"I waited." Until we stop struggling and start trusting, God will never hear or cry. As long as we think that we can save ourselves from the guilt and grip of sin we are doomed to defeat and destruction. So waiting on the Lord suggests utter submission to his saviorhood and sovereignty.

Then, second, there must be *petition*—"He . . . heard
my cry." We are assured that "whosoever shall call upon
the name of the Lord shall be saved [or delivered]" (Rom.
10:13). When Peter began to sink beneath the boisterous
waves he cried, "Lord, save me" (Matt. 14:30), and
instantly the master was there to deliver him and to
restore his faith.

Will you cry right now and know this song of deliverance, this song of direction, and this song of devotion?
This is the song of the new life.

9

The Sense of the New Life
John 10:14–18, 26–30

"My sheep hear my voice, and I know them, and they follow me: and I give unto them eternal life; and they shall
never perish, neither shall any man pluck them out of my
hand. My Father, which gave them me, is greater than all;
and no man is able to pluck them out of my Father's
hand" (10:27–29).

Introduction

Psychologists tell us that one of the strongest instincts
in man is that of self-preservation. Wherever people are
found on the face of the earth they are afraid of insecu-
rity. Talk to any reasonable person and he will share with
you his concern for personal, social, and even for national
security. Indeed, much of our time is spent in insuring
ourselves against poverty, sickness, and death.

There is another dimension of security to which many
people give very little attention. It is that of eternal, or

spiritual, security. The Bible speaks of this again and again throughout its progressive revelation. Paul could say, "I know whom I have believed, and am persuaded that he is able to keep that which I have committed unto him against that day" (2 Tim. 1:12). But the greatest statement on the subject came from our Lord when he declared:

> My sheep hear my voice, and I know them, and they follow me: and I give unto them eternal life; and they shall never perish, neither shall any man pluck them out of my hand. My Father, which gave them me, is greater than all; and no man is able to pluck them out of my Father's hand (10:27–29).

Here he taught that:

I. The Sense of New Life Is a Divine Relationship

Jesus said, "I give unto [my sheep] . . . eternal life" (10:28). When the Savior specifically underscored the words, "my sheep" and "eternal life," he was presupposing a divine relationship. It is described in this passage as:

A. A Personal Relationship

"I give unto [my sheep] . . . eternal life" (10:28). The gospel of Jesus Christ is the gospel of eternal life. It is for this very purpose that the Savior came into the world. As we read, in this very context, he could look into the faces of men and women and say, "I am come that they might have life, and that they might have it more abundantly" (10:10). And John in his epistle reminds us that "this is the record, that God hath given to us eternal life, and this life is in his Son. He that hath the Son hath life; and he that hath not the Son of God hath not life" (1 John 5:11–12). And so we see that this divine relationship involves a living union with Jesus Christ.

Amplification

Amplify how this relationship takes place, by using such verses as John 1:12–13; Revelation 3:20, etc.

B. A Permanent Relationship

"I give unto [my sheep] . . . eternal life; and they shall never perish" (10:28). There are two vital truths in this statement. The first concerns the word "eternal." The term denotes not only a quality of life, but also a quantity of life. In quality, this eternal life is part of the very nature of God. By receiving eternal life we become "partakers of the divine nature" (2 Peter 1:4). But this life is also enduring and endless. Indeed, the mind begins to reel when we try to think of the lastingness of the life which Jesus gives.

Illustration

Stephen Olford recounts: I remember talking to my son, Jonathan, after he had received Christ into his life. I asked him if he were sure that he had received eternal life and he answered "Yes." Then I asked him how long this life would last, and he replied "forever." But I insisted further, "How long is forever?" to which he had no answer. In an effort to illustrate how we might conceive of the length of eternal life, I said, "Think of all the leaves on all the trees in the world. Count them all up and multiply them by a billion. Then number all the grains of sand on all the beaches of the oceans and multiply that total by a billion. Next, calculate how many drops of water there are in all the rivers and oceans and multiply that by a billion. Add your figures together and that would only be the beginning of eternal life." Jonathan's only remark was, "That's a *long* time."

This permanent relationship is also strengthened by the second thought, which is expressed in the words, "I give unto [my sheep] . . . eternal life; and they shall never perish" (10:28). In the Greek, that is expressed by a double negative, which is the strongest positive you can find in Scripture. The word "perish" is a solemn word which carries the idea of ruination and purposelessness. A person who perishes not only deteriorates, but fails to fulfill the purpose for which he was created. This can happen in time, but through a living relationship to Jesus Christ we cease to perish, and enter into the fullness of eternal life.

Amplification

Amplify the conditions that determine eternal security.

II. The Sense of New Life Is a Divine Reliability

"My sheep hear my voice, and I know them, and they follow me" (10:27). Jesus teaches us in these words that the reliability of eternal security is contingent upon:

A. The Authority of His Word

"My sheep hear my voice" (10:27). Whenever the Savior opened his mouth the scribes and Pharisees, and all men and women, were astonished at his doctrine, because he spoke as one having authority (Mark 1:22). We can rely on what he has to say about our eternal security. He declared: "Heaven and earth shall pass away, but my words shall not pass away" (Matt. 24:35). And again: "The Scripture cannot be broken" (John 10:35). And his message to your heart and mine is simply this: "My sheep hear my voice, and I know them, and they follow me: and I give unto them eternal life; and they shall never perish" (10:27–28). What greater reliability can we have than the authority of his Word?

Illustration

Illustrate how this sense of reliability comes through resting upon the Word of God.

B. The Finality of His Work

"My sheep hear my voice, and I know them, and they follow me" (10:27). In that phrase, "I know them," is gathered up the redemptive act by which he has made possible the salvation of every believing man or woman.

Exegesis

Explain verses 14–18 to show what it cost God to secure our salvation.

III. The Sense of New Life Is a Divine Reassurance

"I give unto [my sheep] . . . eternal life; and they shall never perish, neither shall any man pluck them out of my hand. My Father, which gave them me, is greater than all; and no man is able to pluck them out of my Father's hand" (10:28–29). Two hands are referred to in these verses. The one is the Savior's hand, and the other is the Father's hand. How completely reassuring it is to know that once we become related to the Son of God we are held not only by the hand of our wonderful Shepherd, but also by the hand of our heavenly Father. Notice the significance of these hands:

A. The Savior's Hand of Saving Grace

"I give unto [my sheep] . . . eternal life; and they shall never perish, neither shall any man pluck them out of my hand" (10:28). This is the pierced hand that has been stretched out to lay hold of us in saving grace.

Illustration

Holman Hunt has beautifully depicted this aspect of the saving grace of Jesus. He has painted the Good Shepherd bending over a precipitous rock in order to lift the lost and wounded sheep from imminent danger and death. As you examine the picture, you can see the marks on his hands and feet from the thorns and briars. Love and tenderness are written all over his face. But the supreme message of the painting is that of the firm grip of the Shepherd's saving hand. Here is true security!

B. The Father's Hand of Sovereign Choice

"My Father, which gave them me, is greater than all; and no man is able to pluck them out of my Father's hand. I and my Father are one" (10:29–30). Here is a glorious fact. Long before the worlds were thrown into orbit, and the universe was established by an act of the divine will, God, in sovereign grace, chose everyone who would respond to the call of the Shepherd's voice. Paul puts it succinctly when he says,

> Blessed be the God and Father of our Lord Jesus Christ, who hath blessed us with all spiritual blessings in heavenly places in Christ: according as he hath chosen us in him before the foundation of the world, that we should be holy and without blame before him in love (Eph. 1:3–4).

If God in his foreknowledge has laid his hand upon me, can I have any doubt whatsoever about eternal security?

Illustration

Evangelist Tom Rees tells of an occasion when he led a dear lad from the slums of London to a saving experience of Jesus Christ. The time came for the boy to return to his difficult home and surroundings. To give the boy some reassurance, the evangelist read the verses we have been considering and explained something of the meaning of that safe hand of Jesus Christ. "But," remarked the boy, with typical wit, "supposing I slip through his fingers?" "Ah, but that's impossible!" said Tom Rees, "for when the Savior laid hold of you, you *became* one of His fingers!"

Conclusion

Here, then, is the offer of eternal security. Will you receive Christ and enter into the joy of this living and lasting relationship? Then you can sing:

His for ever, only His:
Who the Lord and me shall part?
Ah, with what a rest of bliss
Christ can fill the loving heart.
Heaven and earth may fade and flee,
First-born light in gloom decline;
But, while God and I shall be,
I am His, and He is mine.

W. Robinson

10

The Signs of the New Life
1 John 2:29; 3:9; 4:7; 5:1, 4, 18

"If ye know that he is righteous, ye know that every one that doeth righteousness is born of him. . . . Beloved, let us love one another: for love is of God; and every one that loveth is born of God, and knoweth God. . . . Whosoever believeth that Jesus is the Christ is born of God: and every one that loveth him that begat loveth him also that is begotten of him" (2:29; 4:7; 5:1).

Introduction

Scientists tell us that "life is correspondence to environment." This is true of all forms of life. Where there is no correspondence (that is, no outward expression of life) there is death. The New Testament has a lot to say about the signs of this new life. The apostle John in his first epistle helps us to understand three important evidences of being born again:

80

I. A New Certainty in Christ

"Whosoever believeth that Jesus is the Christ is born of God" (5:1). Believing means more than just an intellectual assent to the facts concerning the Messiahship of Jesus. The apostle James tells us that "the [demons] . . . also believe, and tremble" (James 2:19). In other words, there are no unbelievers in hell. The essential difference is that their intellectual belief never became a saving faith in Jesus Christ. When a person truly believes, in the gospel sense, Christian certainty follows, and our text says, "Whosoever believeth that Jesus is the Christ is born of God" (5:1).

The title "Christ" is important here. It means "Messiah" or "Anointed One." It is a term which applied to prophets (Ps. 105:15), priests (Lev. 4:3) and kings (Ps. 2:2) in Old Testament times. When applied to the Lord Jesus, the title encompasses all these offices in one complete and infinite sense, for as Prophet, Priest, and King, Christ transcends the prophets, priests, and kings of all the ages.

Amplification

Amplify these three offices to show the certainty of the revelation of Christ as prophet, the mediation of Christ as priest, and the supervision of Christ as King.

II. A New Loyalty to Christ

"Every one that loveth is born of God" (4:7). And the apostle John leaves us in no doubt as to how such love expresses itself. To be born of God means:

A. A Loyalty of Love to the Son of God

"We love him, because he first loved us" (4:19). To know experientially what it means to be born again is to fall in love with the Son of God. Love has been defined as the desire for and delight in the person and interests of the one loved. When applied to Jesus

Christ, this means a desire for, and a delight in, the person and purposes of the Son of God.

Illustration

A missionary was once visiting the Yorkshire moors in England. While there, he was told of a godly old shepherd who had been minding the sheep on those moors. The missionary wanted to meet the old man and started to look for him. He soon found him among his sheep, and walking up to him said, "Brother, may I shake hands with you? I hear you love the Lord Jesus." "Yes, sir," replied the shepherd, "I love the Lord Jesus, and me and him's very thick." Could you say that? Are you on such intimate terms with the Lord Jesus?

B. A Loyalty of Love to the Word of God

"Whoso keepeth his word, in him verily is the love of God perfected" (2:5). Love for God must always be measured by obedience to his Word. The Savior summed this up when he said, "If ye love me, keep my commandments" (John 14:15). King David's profound regard for the Word of God is beautifully expressed in the longest Psalm he ever wrote. He says, "O how love I thy law! it is my meditation all the day"; and again: "I love thy commandments above gold; yea, above fine gold" (119:97, 127).

Amplification

Amplify by developing such questions as, Do you value the Word of God? Do you read it, obey it, live it, and preach it?

C. A Loyalty of Love to the Church of God

"Every one that loveth him that begat loveth him also that is begotten of him" (5:1). This means that if we are truly born again we cannot help loving those who share our common life in Christ. Jesus said, "By this shall all men know that ye are my disciples, if ye have love one to another" (John 13:35). Such love must not be confused with sentimentality or infatuation. On the contrary, it is a very sacrificial (1 John 3:16) and practical (1 John 3:17) thing.

Illustration

In an engine room it is impossible to look into the great boiler and see how much water it contains. But attached to the boiler is a tiny glass tube which serves as a gauge. As the water stands in the little tube, so it stands in the great boiler. When the tube is half full, the boiler is half full; when the tube is empty, the boiler is empty. If you want to know how much you love God, look at the gauge. *Your love for your brother* is the measure of your love for God.

III. A New Victory in Christ

"Every one that *doeth* righteousness is born of him" (2:29). By nature, we are incapable of doing righteousness. The Bible says, "There is none righteous, no, not one. . . . there is none that doeth good" (Rom. 3:10, 12). But when the miracle of the new birth takes place all that is changed; we become "partakers of the divine nature" (2 Peter 1:4), and instead of living defeated lives we begin to live victorious lives. We enjoy:

A. Victory over Sin

"Whosoever is born of God doth not commit sin" (1 John 3:9). The better reading here is "Whosoever is born of God does not practice sin." In other words, a born-again person does not continue willfully in sin because he is possessed of a divine nature which abhors sin. Therefore, as he feeds the new nature and counts upon it for victory, he finds it to be the liberating power of God over his old sinful nature. Thereafter, failure only occurs when the old nature is allowed to dominate; otherwise, it is victory all along the way!

Illustration

Illustrate how to starve the old nature and how to feed the new.

B. Victory over Self

"[Whosoever] is born of God overcometh the world" (5:4). In this epistle John teaches that the world, for the believer, is the lust of the flesh, the lust of the eyes, and the pride of life (1 John 2:16). In a word, this is self—that subtle, assertive ego within us which mars the home, splits the church, and ruins the world. So a very evident sign of the new life is the indwelling power which conquers the self-life. This involves more than overcoming sin. Sin is the outcome of conceived lust. So, to conquer and control the inner self-life is to forestall sin in its outworking. This victory which overcomes the self-life is the faith which hands over the lust and pride of our self-centeredness to the control of the indwelling Christ.

C. Victory over Satan

"Whosoever is born of God sinneth not; but he that is begotten of God keepeth himself, and that wicked one toucheth him not" (5:18). Here is the supreme mark of the new life. Very simply, it is overcoming the evil one. Satan may and does assault, but he need never hold us down. We can defeat him through faith in the indwelling Son of God who was manifested "that he might destroy the works of the devil" (3:8). Every truly born-again person can say with confidence, "Greater is he that is in . . . [me], than he that is in the world" (4:4).

Conclusion

Here, then, are the vital signs of new life in Christ: first, a certainty in Christ; second, a loyalty to Christ; and third, a victory in Christ. Are these signs evident in your life or are you living a lie? If so, quit shamming and trust Christ as your prophet, priest, and King. Open the door of your heart and let him in and trust him to reproduce in you the signs of his new life.

11

The Steps of the New Life
Romans 6:1–14

"Therefore we are buried with him by baptism into death: that like as Christ was raised up from the dead by the glory of the Father, even so we also should walk in newness of life" (6:4).

Introduction

Many figures of speech are used to describe the Christian life. Sometimes it is called a fight, and we think of the soldier in his armor with a sword in his hand. Or the Christian is depicted as an athlete—boxing or running. But perhaps the most frequent picture is that of a walker. Seven times over in the Epistle to the Ephesians the believer is told how to *walk* in Christ. The walk suggests action, direction, and destination. The important thing about a walk, however, is that it is the extension of a step. Every journey starts with the first step, and we must never forget that. Paul reminds us that "as [we] . . . have

... received Christ Jesus the Lord, so [we are to] walk ... in him" and again, we are to: "walk in newness of life" (Col. 2:6; Rom. 6:4). From Romans 6 we learn about:

I. The Steps in the New Life of Liberation

"He that is dead is freed from sin" (6:7). This chapter opens with a question, "Shall we continue in sin, that grace may abound?" (6:1). In other words, is the grace of God an excuse for sinning? Now this is an important issue that we must face if we are to understand the new life in Christ. There are those who believe that as long as they confess their sins to a priest, or a pastor, they can live as they please. Paul condemns this outright. He exclaims, "God forbid. How shall we, that are dead to sin, live any longer therein?" (6:2). In other words, the pathway of liberation is not to continue in sin, but rather to live in victory. And so he declares, "He that is dead is freed from sin" (6:7).

A. The Death of Christ Brings Liberty from the Penalty of Sin

"Know ye not, that so many of us as were baptized into Jesus Christ were baptized into his death?" (6:3). To be united to Jesus Christ through simple faith is to be free from the penalty of sin. Christ died for our sins in order that we might not die. He took the punishment we deserved in order that we might not be punished. To understand this is to be liberated from the wages of sin.

Illustration

Behind the platform of Faneuil Hall, Boston, stands a large painting of Webster's debate with Hayne inscribed "Union and Liberty, one and inseparable, now and forever." Preaching in this hall, General William Booth concluded his sermon with a dramatic peroration. Turning to

the painting, he cried: "'Union and liberty'—unity with
Christ and liberty from sin—'one and inseparable, now and
forever!'" The one standard against sin's thralldom is
union with the living Christ. There is no spiritual liberty
apart from this union.

B. The Death of Christ Brings Liberty
from the Cruelty of Sin

"Therefore we are buried with him by baptism into
death" (6:4). The Lord Jesus was not only put to death,
he was also buried. This is why Paul spells out the
gospel by saying, "Christ died for our sins according to
the scriptures; and that he was buried, and that he rose
again the third day according to the scriptures" (1 Cor.
15:3–4). This matter of Christ's burial is often over-
looked in our preaching, but in Paul's mind there was
clearly a divine purpose in the burial of Christ. Not
only did it certify his death, and therefore enhance the
full significance of his resurrection, but it robbed sin of
its cruelty. The grave is a cruel place. Solomon says
that "jealousy is cruel as the grave" (Song of Sol. 8:6),
but since the burial of Christ we can say with Paul, "O
death, where is thy sting? O grave, where is thy victory?" (1 Cor. 15:55). To be united with Christ by faith
in his burial is to be liberated from the cruelty of sin.

C. The Death of Christ Brings Liberty
from the Slavery of Sin

"Like as Christ was raised up from the dead by the
glory of the Father, even so we also should walk in
newness of life. . . . Knowing this, that our old man is
crucified with him, that the body of sin might be
destroyed, that henceforth we should not serve sin"
(6:4, 6). The secret of victory over sin in all of its subtle
and multiple forms is that we can be united by faith to
a Christ who rose from the dead to become our
indwelling Savior and deliverer. This is what Paul
means when he says, "I am crucified with Christ: never-

theless I live; yet not I, but Christ liveth in me" (Gal. 2:20). By his indwelling power Christ can save us, moment by moment, from the slavery of sin.

Illustration

Madam Guyon wrote prolifically in prison in France for her Savior's sake. This cultured, refined, educated, and (until smitten with smallpox) exceedingly beautiful woman spent ten years of her life in various French prisons between 1695–1705. Here are some of her words:

> My cage confines me round;
> Abroad I cannot fly;
> But though my wing is closely bound,
> My heart's at liberty.
> My prison walls cannot control
> The flight, the freedom of the soul.
> Oh, it's good to soar
> These bolts and bars above,
> To Him whose purpose I adore,
> Whose providence I love;
> And in Thy mighty will to find
> The joy, the freedom of the mind.

II. The Steps in the New Life of Dedication

"Yield yourselves unto God, as those that are alive from the dead, and your members as instruments of righteousness unto God" (6:13). Paul is here using language that would be well understood by his readers in Rome, a city filled with wickedness, corruption, and sin. He makes clear that the steps of the new life of dedication must involve two things:

A. The Dethronement of Sin

"Let not sin therefore reign in your mortal body, that ye should obey it in the lusts thereof" (6:12). Personifying sin as a king, the apostle says, "Don't let sin reign in your mortal body." In other words, set your mind, heart, and will against the attempt of sin to occupy the throne of your heart. This does not mean that we lose our sinful nature while here upon earth. That will happen only when we get to heaven; but it does teach that sin must no longer have dominion over us (6:14). Sin may be dormant but it need not be dominant; sin may be the slave in our lives without being the master. But we must resolutely determine that sin will not rule and reign in our hearts and lives.

Illustration

A father and his small son were walking one evening in the quiet village. Suddenly the boy's voice piped, "Daddy, don't look, just come closer to me, 'cause there's something dirty on the sidewalk." Isn't that a lesson for us Christians as we walk through this defiled world! We know things are there—vain things, unclean things, filthy things. God tells us they are in the world—but we don't have to *look* at them. Just as that boy refused to be contaminated with the filth of the sidewalk, so we must dethrone sin in our lives.

B. The Enthronement of God

"Yield yourselves unto God" (6:13). This is both an initial act and a continual attitude. It is the handing over of our total personalities to the sovereignty and authority of God in our lives.

Illustration

Stephen Olford recounts: I remember so clearly when this happened in my own life. I had been a Christian for some time, but had never understood the meaning of full surrender until God showed me the utter wastefulness and uselessness of a life lived for self. Jesus Christ is Lord, whether we like to admit it or not, and he will see to it that we submit to that Lordship, even if it means chastening us, in order to make us what he wants us to be. Only when God is enthroned in the person of his Son, Jesus Christ, can we know true deliverance and victory. Let me ask you: Is every part of your life yielded—your spirit, soul, and body? The verse says, "Yield yourselves unto God . . . and your members as instruments of righteousness unto God" (6:13). That means your eyes, your ears, your lips, your hands, your feet, your all.

These are the important steps in the life of dedication—the dethronement of self and the enthronement of God.

III. The Steps in the New Life of Occupation

"But now being made free from sin, and become servants to God, ye have your fruit unto holiness, and the end everlasting life" (6:22). Having declared that the Christian is a liberated and dedicated person, Paul proceeds to show that the Christian is someone who occupies his time in the service of the kingdom. So he points out further steps in the new life of occupation:

A. A Loyal Servant Must Own His Master

"Know ye not, that to whom ye yield yourselves servants to obey, his servants ye are to whom ye obey; whether of sin unto death, or of obedience unto righteousness?" (6:16). Quite clearly, two masters are personified in the words "sin" and "obedience." As servants, we must choose our master and then serve him. If we choose Christ, then we must serve him and no other. Jesus laid down this principle when he declared, "No man can serve two masters" (Matt. 6:24). The tragedy is that so many Christians have this double loyalty. Instead of accepting their union with Christ in death, burial, and resurrection, and therefore rejoicing in their liberty in Christ for service and fruitfulness, they become spurners of the grace of God and shirkers in the church of God. The true servant of Jesus Christ is the person who has declared, before witnesses, that he is committed to his master forever.

Illustration

Illustrate the master/servant relationship as recorded in Exodus 21:1–6.

B. A Loyal Servant Must Obey His Master

"But God be thanked, that ye were the servants of sin, but ye have obeyed from the heart that form of doctrine which was delivered [unto] you" (6:17). In the Greek New Testament there are six words which are translated "servant," and it is significant that the one Paul selects to describe the believer in this passage is the term translated "slave" or "bondslave." Without doubt, Paul had in mind the thousands of slaves who were in the city of Rome. To such, the very word would stir up a sense of horror if used without some qualification. But in these verses Paul takes up this word and associates it with the Lord Jesus Christ. The Savior called himself the bondslave of God. So the apostle loved to call himself a bondslave of Jesus Christ. In this sense, Paul not only retrieved the word, but redeemed it. He took all the bitterness out of it, not only for the slaves of Rome, but for every Christian throughout succeeding centuries. When he speaks of obedience to the Master he means an obedience of love.

Amplification

Show that obedience must be rendered in terms of doctrine (6:17) and duty (6:22).

Conclusion

So we see what it means to walk in newness of life. It involves steps in the life of liberation, dedication, and occupation. Have you started this walk? Remember, it begins with the first step—stepping out of yourself into Christ. This means repentance, faith, and obedience— turning from yourself, trusting in Christ, and then taking this new life of Christian liberation, dedication, and occupation. Will you take this step right now? If you will, new life will truly begin.

12

The Strength of the New Life
Philippians 4:1–13

"I can do all things through Christ which strengtheneth me" (4:13).

Introduction

This is one of the most exciting verses in all the Bible. Paul is in prison, chained to soldiers, and awaiting trial and impending death. In spite of these circumstances, however, he could write one of his happiest letters and conclude with the words that we have chosen for our text. He says:

> I have learned, in whatsoever state I am, therewith to be content. I know both how to be abased, and I know how to abound: every where and in all things I am instructed both to be full and to be hungry, both to abound and to suffer need. *I can do all things through Christ which strengtheneth me* (4:11–13).

Paul had discovered the strength of new life in Christ. In every situation and circumstance he had proved Christ to be more than adequate; indeed, he claimed he could do all things through Christ who strengthened him.

Here is a secret we cannot afford to overlook or ignore. Let us examine Paul's statement and find out what was, in fact, the supernatural secret that he discovered in Christ.

I. The Strength of a Satisfied Life in Christ

"I have learned, in whatsoever state I am, therewith to be content" (4:11). Contentment in Christ was the reward of spiritual discipline. No matter what state Paul was in, he was content because he knew how to apply the laws of spiritual discipline. He accepted adversity with cheerful resignation, he respected prosperity with careful moderation; in both states he was content because his ultimate satisfaction was centered in Christ. His attitude toward life is beautifully summed up in the words we find in the Hebrew epistle: "Be content with such things as ye have: for he hath said, I will never leave thee, nor forsake thee" (13:5). His contentment was not an insensible stoicism, but rather a disciplined adjustment to life, by the power of the indwelling Christ.

Illustration

The story is told of a child of wealthy parents who was brought to a wonderful old Christian who lived in abject poverty. For a few moments he looked at the little girl. Then gently stroking her lovely blonde curls he said, "My child, may God make this world as beautiful to you as it has been to me." Like Paul, this dear old saint knew the secret and strength of satisfaction in Christ.

A. Physical Satisfaction in Christ

"I have learned, in whatsoever state I am, therewith to be content" (4:11). Let us remember that Paul carried to his death an affliction which he described as "a thorn in the flesh" (2 Cor. 12:7), and yet he triumphed.

Amplification

Expound on 2 Corinthians 12:7–9.

B. Spiritual Satisfaction in Christ

"I have learned, in whatsoever state I am, therewith to be content" (4:11). Earlier in this same letter he could say, "For me to live is Christ" (1:21), or more literally, "For me, living itself is Christ." He knew the difference between living and existing.

Illustration

A bishop was contented and cheerful through a long period of trial and was asked the secret of his contentment. He said, "I will tell you. I made right use of my eyes." "Please explain." "Most willingly," was the answer.

First I look up to heaven and remember that my principal business is to get there. Then I look down upon the earth and think how small a place I shall occupy when I am dead and buried. Then I look around and see the many who are in all respects much worse off than I am. Then I remember where true happiness lies, where all our cares end, and how little reason I have to complain.

The bishop had learned in whatsoever state he was, therewith to be content.

II. The Strength of an Edified Life in Christ

He says: "I know both how to be abased, and I know how to abound: every where and in all things *I am instructed* both to be full and to be hungry, both to abound and to suffer need" (4:12). Literally, that sentence reads: "I have been taught the secret." As someone has put it, Paul the slave of Christ was led to a mastery over circumstances which made him a king. He could face adversity, but, more importantly, he could face prosperity.

A. Maturity in Times of Adversity

"I know . . . how to be abased" (4:12). We live in a world where nothing is stable. Overnight we may lose everything we possess. Tragedy may strike because of a tornado, a burglary, a revolution, an atomic bomb, and so on. The question is, are we able to face disasters of this kind with quiet maturity? Have we been edified "both to be full and to be hungry, both to abound and to suffer need" (4:12)? Only as we sit at the feet of Jesus can we learn this secret.

Illustration
Illustrate by using the example of Job (Job 13:15).

B. Humility in Times of Prosperity

"I know how to abound" (4:12). Though Paul dictated this letter in a Roman dungeon, he also knew what it was to live in wealthy homes. Many times he had enjoyed the luxury and hospitality of generous hosts. In certain circles he was one of the most respected men of his day, and yet the extraordinary thing was that he never lost his head. He was so edified in Christ that he knew Christ's humility. Earlier in this epistle he deals with this in great depth and richness. He says: "Let this mind be in you, which was also in Christ Jesus: who, being in the form of God, thought it not robbery to be equal with God: but made himself of no reputation, and took upon him the form of a servant, and was made in the likeness of men: and being found in fashion as a man, he humbled himself, and became obedient unto death, even the death of the cross" (2:5–8).

Illustration
Cite examples from your own experience of those who have been exalted and yet remained humble.

III. The Strength of a Fortified Life in Christ

"I can do all things through Christ which strengtheneth me" (4:13). Another version has it: "I am strong for all things in the One who constantly infuses strength in me" (WUEST). To be able to say and mean "I can do all things through Christ which strengtheneth me" is to know the very essence of Christian living. Although the context here indicates that Paul meant that he was able to cope with any given situation, the principle implicit in this great utterance may be extended to include God's enabling for any and all Christian responsibilities. To know the conscious and continual power of the indwelling Christ guarantees:

A. Strength to Live Faithfully

"Therefore, my brethren . . . stand fast in the Lord" (4:1).

B. Strength to Live Joyfully

"Rejoice in the Lord alway: and again I say, Rejoice" (4:4).

C. Strength to Live Helpfully

"Let your moderation be known unto all men. The Lord is at hand" (4:5). Etymologically, moderation means "that yieldingness which urges not its own rights to the uttermost."

D. Strength to Live Prayerfully

"Be careful for nothing; but in every thing by prayer and supplication with thanksgiving let your requests be made known unto God" (4:6).

E. Strength to Live Thankfully

"With thanksgiving let your requests be made known unto God" (4:6).

F. Strength to Live Peacefully

"And the peace of God which passeth all understanding, shall keep your hearts and minds through Christ Jesus" (4:7).

G. Strength to Live Thoughtfully

"Finally, brethren, whatsoever things are true, whatsoever things are honest, whatsoever things are just, whatsoever things are pure, whatsoever things are lovely, whatsoever things are of good report; if there be any virtue, and if there be any praise, think on these things" (4:8).

Amplification

Amplify these seven points to round off the sermon and illustrate, where necessary.

Conclusion

So the challenge of this message confronts us with the only One in the universe who can satisfy, edify, and fortify our lives with supernatural strength. If you don't know him already in your life, this wonderful Christ stands before you and says, "Behold, I stand at the door, and knock" (Rev. 3:20). If you let him in he will become the very strength of your life—the strength which satisfies, edifies, and fortifies for any situation or circumstance of life. Don't reject him. Rather, accept him and obey him as Savior and Lord of your life.

13

The Scope of the New Life

2 Peter 3:1–14

"Nevertheless we, according to his promise, look for new heavens and a new earth, wherein dwelleth righteousness" (3:13).

Introduction

Millions of people in every land are anxiously looking into the future and wondering what it holds in store for them. Parents are concerned about their children, and young people want to know what awaits them in a world that is confused and desperate. The blind optimism of former days is gone, and thinking people are beginning to see the utter emptiness of any form of human utopianism. Someone recently put it, "A survey of the world leaves one with the uncomfortable feeling that, in spite of the efforts of many well-intentioned men in every country, civilization is sliding downhill." That, in a few sentences, is the story of our modern world. And a hopeless story it is, were it not for the Christian message, for it is into this very context that Peter's words fit with profound significance. "We," says he, "according to . . . [Christ's] promise, look for new heavens and a new earth, wherein dwelleth righteousness" (3:13). God's answer to world chaos is the coming new world. This is the scope of the new life.

I. The Promise of the Coming New World

"We, according to his promise, look for new heavens and a new earth" (3:13). Earlier in this chapter Peter says, "I stir up your pure minds by way of remembrance: that ye may be mindful of the words which were spoken before by the holy prophets, and of the commandment of us the apostles of the Lord and Saviour" (3:1–2). The apostle here reminds his readers that the subject of the coming again of Jesus Christ was no new truth. In general terms, the prophets of old had already foretold it, and it had been described in more specific terms by the apostles who followed. In other words, the promise of the coming new world was both foretold and foreshadowed in Holy Scripture.

A. The Promise Foretold

"The words which were spoken before by the holy prophets" (3:2). From Genesis to Malachi there are no less than 333 direct prophecies concerning our Lord's first coming, and scholars tell us that there are at least double that number relating to his second coming.

Amplification
Draw on Old Testament prophecies to support the second advent.

B. The Promise Foreshadowed

"We, according to his promise, look for new heavens and a new earth" (3:13). Peter answers the scoffers who say, "Where is the promise of his coming? for since the fathers fell asleep, all things continue as they were from the beginning of creation" (3:4). The point which Peter makes three times over is that God is absolutely precise in all his timing.

Amplification

Amplify a) the timing of God's act of creation (3:5); b) the timing of God's act of destruction (3:6); c) the timing of God's act of redemption (3:9).

II. The Purpose of the Coming New World

"We . . . look for new heavens and a new earth, wherein dwelleth righteousness" (3:13). In what is known as the prophetic present, Peter uses language in this paragraph to anticipate the fulfillment of God's prophetic program. In God's purpose for the coming new world Peter sees a threefold design:

A. A Personal Design

"We, according to his promise, look" (3:13). Here we glimpse Christ's personal design to fulfill the expectations of his own people, who look for the new world.

Illustration

At night, as Dr. Horatius Bonar retired to rest, his last action before he lay down to sleep was to draw aside the curtain and look into the starry sky and say, "Perhaps tonight, Lord?" In the morning, as he arose, his first movement was to raise the blinds, look out upon the gray dawn and remark, "Perhaps today, Lord?"

B. A Punitive Design

"New heavens and a new earth" (3:13). This presupposes the dissolving of the old heavens and earth. Until recently, those who talked about the end of the world were termed "cranks" and "religious fanatics." Today, the scoffing has ended. Men have covered their mouths. Indeed, the philosophers, politicians, and scientists themselves have become the prophets of doom.

Illustration

In September, 1946, Sir Winston Churchill (then Mr. Churchill) shook the world with this statement: "It may well be that, in a few years, the atom bomb will not only ring an end to all that we can call civilization, but may disintegrate the globe itself."

Update this prediction with the facts as we know them today.

C. A Permanent Design

"New heavens and a new earth, wherein dwelleth righteousness" (3:13). Christ's permanent design, in the new world, is a lasting habitation of righteousness. "Behold, I make all things new" (Rev. 21:5), he says, and he will surely fulfill his Word.

Illustration

Illustrate how Lot fled to a city of refuge after Sodom and Gomorrah were destroyed by the fires of wrath.

III. The People of the Coming New World

"Seeing then that all these things shall be dissolved, what manner of persons ought ye to be in all holy conversation and godliness, looking for and hasting unto the coming of the day of God" (3:11–12). When Peter says, "What manner of men ought ye to be?" he is describing the people of the new world. The construction of the sentence implies that the state in which such people are to be found is one which has continued for some time before the day arrives.

A. *They Must Be Holy*

"What manner of persons ought ye to be in all holy conversation [or life]" (3:11). Holiness is both a gift and a process. It is a good gift from God in Christ; it is also a process to be worked out in daily life.

Amplification

Expound on such verses as 1 Corinthians 1:30, Hebrews 12:14, and 1 Peter 1:14, 15.

B. *They Must Be Godly*

"What manner of persons ought ye to be in . . . godliness" (3:11). Godliness is the realization of God's abiding presence, resulting in God-likeness.

Amplification

Amplify by using such verses as Psalm 4:3, 2 Timothy 3:12, Titus 2:12, Hebrews 12:28, etc.

C. *They Must Be Busy*

"What manner of persons ought ye to be . . . looking for and hasting unto the coming of the day of God" (3:11–12). There is no "unto" in the original. The sense of the verse is rather "hastening the coming" (NKJV) by winning souls to Christ through the spread of the gospel.

Amplification

Amplify the ways and means by which we could speed the work of the gospel.

Conclusion

The world stands on the brink of total destruction. Some time ago, in an address, a leading statesman said: "At least 90 percent of all Americans now living will be killed by atomic bombs within the near future." The accuracy of that statement has not yet been proven, but one thing is clear:

> The world is very evil,
> The times are waxing late;
> Be sober, then, and watchful—
> The Judge is at the gate!

Are you going to be judged and destroyed with the old world, or are you going to be saved and included in the new world? Oh, that your response might be:

> Make me holy by Thy blood,
> Make me godly, Lamb of God;
> Keep me busy in the fray,
> Make me ready for "that day."

> Stephen F. Olford

Endnotes

Chapter 1

1. Adapted and reprinted from *The Word for Every Day* by Alvin N. Rogness, copyright © 1981 Augsburg Publishing House, p. 156. Used by permission of Augsburg Fortress.

2. Paul R. Van Gorder, *Our Daily Bread* (Grand Rapids: Radio Bible Class), adapted.

Chapter 2

1. Ralph Waldo Emerson, quoted in Paul Lee Tan, *Encyclopedia of 7,700 Illustrations* (Dallas: Bible Communications, 1979), p. 647.

2. Henry G. Bosch, quoted in ibid.

3. Copyright 1915. Renewal 1943 by Hope Publishing Company, Carol Stream, Illinois. All rights reserved. Used by permission.

Chapter 3

1. Paul Lee Tan, *Encyclopedia of 7,700 Illustrations* (Dallas: Bible Communications, 1979), p. 186.

2. Copyrighted, March 4, 1982 Chicago Tribune Company, all rights reserved, used with permission.

Chapter 4

1. James Montgomery Boice, *Does Inerrancy Matter?* Published by the International Council on Biblical Inerrancy and used by permission of Evangelical Ministries, Inc., 1716 Spruce Street, Philadelphia, PA 19103.

For Further Reading

Part 1: Christian Evidence

Anderson, James Norman Dalrymple. *Jesus Christ: The Witness of History.* Downers Grove, Ill.: InterVarsity Press, 1984.

Anderson, Robert. *The Lord from Heaven.* Grand Rapids: Kregel Publications, 1978.

Bavinck, Herman. *The Doctrine of God.* Trans. William Hendriksen. Edinburgh: Banner of Truth Trust, 1977.

Baxter, James Sidlow. *Majesty: The God You Should Know.* San Bernardino, Calif.: Here's Life Publishers, 1984.

Blailock, E. M. *Jesus Christ, Man or Myth?* Nashville: Thomas Nelson Publishers, 1984.

Boice, James Montgomery. *The Sovereign God.* Vol. 1. Foundations of the Christian Faith. Downers Grove, Ill.: InterVarsity Press, 1978.

———. *Standing on the Rock.* Wheaton, Ill.: Tyndale House Publishers, 1984.

Bruce, F. F. *Jesus and Christian Origins Outside the New Testament.* Grand Rapids: Wm. B. Eerdmans Publishing Co., 1974.

Carroll, Benajah Harvey. *Inspiration of the Bible.* Nashville: Thomas Nelson Publishers, 1980.

Clark, Gordon Haddon. *God's Hammer: The Bible and Its Critics.* Jefferson, Md.: Trinity Foundation, 1982.

———. *The Trinity.* Jefferson, Md.: Trinity Foundation, 1985.

France, R. T. *The Living God.* Downers Grove, Ill.: InterVarsity Press, 1973.

Haldane, Robert. *The Authenticity and Inspiration of the Holy Scriptures.* Minneapolis: Klock and Klock Christian Publishers, 1985.

Hogan, Ronald F. *The God of Glory.* Neptune, N.J.: Loizeaux Brothers, Inc., 1984.

Law, Peter W. *A Portrait of My Father: The Wonder of Knowing God.* Portland, Oreg.: Multnomah Press, 1985.

Lawlor, George. *When God Became Man.* Chicago: Moody Press, 1978.

Liddon, Henry Parry. *The Divinity of Our Lord and Saviour Jesus Christ.* Minneapolis: Klock and Klock Christian Publishers, 1978.

Lightner, Robert Paul. *The First Fundamental: God.* Nashville: Thomas Nelson Publishers, 1973.

―――. *The God of the Bible: An Introduction to the Doctrine of God.* Grand Rapids: Baker Book House, 1978.

Lindsell, Harold. *The Battle for the Bible.* Grand Rapids: Zondervan Publishing House, 1976.

MacArthur, John F., Jr. *Why Believe the Bible?* Ventura, Calif.: Regal Books, 1980.

M'Intosh, Hugh. *Is Christ Infallible and the Bible True?* Minneapolis: Klock and Klock Christian Publishers, 1981.

Morris, Henry M. *The Genesis Record: A Scientific and Devotional Commentary on the Book of Beginnings.* Grand Rapids: Baker Book House, 1976.

Packer, James I. *Knowing God.* Downers Grove, Ill.: InterVarsity Press, 1973.

Radmacher, Earl D., ed. *Can We Trust the Bible?* Wheaton, Ill.: Tyndale House Publishers, 1979.

Robertson, A. T. *The Divinity of Christ in the Gospel of John.* 1916. Reprint. 1 vol. Grand Rapids: Zondervan Publishing House, 1975.

Sanders, J. Oswald. *The Incomparable Christ.* Chicago: Moody Press, 1971.

Saphir, Adolph. *Divine Unity of Scripture.* Grand Rapids:

Kregel Publications, 1984.

Smail, Thomas Allan. *The Forgotten Father.* Grand Rapids: Wm. B. Eerdmans Publishing Co., 1981.

Stott, John R. W. *The Authentic Jesus: The Centrality of Christ in a Skeptical World.* Downers Grove, Ill.: InterVarsity Press, 1985.

Tenney, Merrill C. *John: The Gospel of Belief.* Grand Rapids: Wm. B. Eerdmans Publishing Co., 1969.

Toon, Peter. *God Here and Now: The Christian View of God.* Wheaton, Ill.: Tyndale House Publishers, 1979.

Toon, Peter, and James D. Spiceland, eds. *One God in Trinity.* Westchester, Ill.: Cornerstone Books, 1980.

Vine, W. E. *The Divine Sonship of Christ.* 2 vols. in 1. Minneapolis: Klock and Klock Christian Publishers, 1984.

Part 2: New Life for You

Anderson, Robert. *Redemption Truths.* Grand Rapids: Kregel Publications, 1980.

Barker, Harold. *Secure Forever.* Neptune, N.J.: Loizeaux Brothers, Inc., 1974.

Baxter, James Sidlow. *God So Loved.* Grand Rapids: Zondervan Publishing House, 1960.

———. *His Part and Ours.* Grand Rapids: Zondervan Publishing House, 1964.

Boice, James Montgomery. *Awakening to God.* Vol. 3. Foundations of the Christian Life. Downers Grove, Ill.: InterVarsity Press, 1979.

Chafer, Lewis Sperry. *Grace.* Grand Rapids: Zondervan Publishing House, 1965.

———. *Salvation.* Grand Rapids: Zondervan Publishing House, 1965.

Clark, Gordon Haddon. *Faith and Saving Faith.* Jefferson, Md.: Trinity Foundation, 1983.

Denney, James. *The Biblical Doctrine of Reconciliation.* Minneapolis: Klock and Klock Christian Publishers, 1985.

Erickson, Millard John, ed. *Salvation: God's Amazing Plan.* Wheaton, Ill.: Victor Books, 1978.

Graham, William Franklin. *Peace with God.* Waco, Tex.: Word Books, 1984.

Gromacki, Robert Glenn. *Salvation Is Forever.* Chicago: Moody Press, 1974.

Holliday, John Francis. *Life From Above: The Need for Emphasis on Biblical Regeneration.* London: Marshall, Morgan & Scott, 1957.

Horne, Charles M. *Salvation.* Chicago: Moody Press, 1971.

Hoyt, Herman Arthur. *Expository Messages on the New Birth.* Grand Rapids: Baker Book House, 1961.

Kevan, Ernest Frederick. *Salvation.* Grand Rapids: Baker Book House, 1963.